Abstinent Cook
for
Food Addicts

MW01056530

Food Addicts Anonymous
Approved Literature

Food Addicts Anonymous, Inc.
529 NW Prima Vista Blvd., #301A
Port St. Lucie, FL 34983
http://www.foodaddictsanonymous.org
info@foodaddictsanonymous.org

Sixth Edition
Second Printing
© Revised 2010, 2004, 2003, 2001, 1997, 1995
ISBN 978-09638074-34

9 780963 807434

In Gratitude

We wish to express our gratitude to the many food addicts who unselfishly took the time to share their recipes with us. Our added thanks go to those who helped eliminate foods that might compromise someone's abstinence.

"Abstinent Cooking for Food Addicts" is intended to make our abstinence easier. To those who typed and edited the copy over and over again...your service is priceless and without you this cookbook would never have become a reality. Your generosity of time and talent has enabled the hand of Food Addicts Anonymous to reach out in a new and more complete way, for even the most novice of cooks.

TABLE OF CONTENTS

SEVENTH STEP PRAYER

God, help me listen to my Higher Self as You and I make the changes in my life that will allow me to live a free, useful and happy life. Help me to not find fault with all that I do and with those who cross my path. As I continue to stay abstinent, help me be released from the cravings for foods that are not in my best interest. Help me learn that food is to nourish my body so my spirit can carry out your plans for me. Help me be compassionate, trusting, forgiving, loving and kind to myself and others as I serve you and the people on earth. Amen. (The FAA Steps to Recovery, 1992).

OUR PRIMARY PURPOSE

Food Addicts Anonymous is a fellowship of men and women who are willing to recover from the disease of food addiction. Sharing our experience, strength, and hope with others allows us to recover from this disease, One Day at a Time.

Food Addicts Anonymous is self-supporting through our own contributions. We are not affiliated with any diet or weight loss programs, treatment facilities or religious organizations. We neither endorse nor oppose any causes. Our primary purpose is to stay abstinent and help other food addicts to achieve abstinence.

FIRST THINGS FIRST

We suggest you read "A Guide to Abstinence" thoroughly to help you understand how to recover physically from the disease of food addiction. We also suggest you study the "Names of Sugar," which includes names of flours and wheat, to help you avoid these substances. We also have a Daily Food Diary which will help you avoid repeating the same foods, perhaps creating an allergic reaction. This food diary will also aid in grocery shopping, relief from boredom with your meals and keep you on the physical path to recovery. Our cookbook is an aid to make life easier. We want to share our recipes so you can look forward to staying abstinent without feeling deprived. Food doesn't have to be tasteless or unappetizing to be abstinent. We are not interested in being martyrs, just abstinent. Our meals can be tasteful, colorful, appetizing and healthy by following a few simple directions. **To recover, it is paramount that we abstain from sugar, flour and wheat and eliminate all forms of artificial sweeteners.**

As food addicts we have a 3-fold disease, physical, emotional and mental, all of which make us spiritual beings. We use all the tools at our disposal to attain recovery. We can attend or start a meeting, work our Twelve Steps and Twelve Traditions, sponsor a newcomer, share with each other from our wealth of experience, and serve ourselves while we serve others.

WHO IS A FOOD ADDICT?

When we lose control of our lives and can no longer define reality, despair becomes our daily companion. How many times have we attempted to satisfy our soul needs with food, only to find the same emptiness within? As our self-esteem disappeared and our health worsened, we searched frantically for a way out. Diets became our Higher Power, only to fail us again and again. Fear filled us; we became isolated in a room full of people. With abstinence from sugar, flour, wheat and other high carbohydrate foods, we can find hope to live our lives. Our Higher Power leads us forward with love to freedom to a happy useful life. Abstinence will open the door, and by working the Twelve Steps, we can recover from this disease.

DEFINITION OF ABSTINENCE

We ask for help from our Higher Power to abstain from those substances we find ourselves craving, ever mindful of our addiction to sugar, flour and wheat. Feeding our bodies with a plan of sound nutrition will allow us freedom from the insanity of this disease. With honesty, an open mind and willingness to share our experience, strength and hope, we can recover from this disease... **ONE DAY AT A TIME.**

"THE GUIDE TO ABSTINENCE"

GUIDELINES FOR THE FAA MEAL PLAN
Abstinence is a Commitment to Recovery

Of course, to the newly recovering person, this appears as another diet. But we who walk this path of recovery know that this program of eating is unique.

One of the obstacles you may encounter in early recovery is the temptation to alter the food plan to suit yourself. It is our experience that deviations recreate our old food problems. To guard yourself against the tendency to rationalize, it is suggested that you discuss any additions or subtractions you may think are necessary with a sponsor or someone in the program who is abstinent.

1. Weigh or measure all food as specified. Volume can trigger the disease. Eating larger or smaller quantities of food than recommended on the food plan can cause the physical cravings to reappear and can lead us back into the disease of food addiction. Eating added volume or restricting is often the beginning of the relapse process. Invest in measuring cups, measuring spoons and a good scale. Since this is NOT a diet, wide variety and attractive presentation of your meals will help you stay abstinent. Make it interesting!

2. Look for hidden or additional names of sugar, flour and wheat in the "Ingredient" section of the label on all packaged or canned foods, drinks, marinades, dressings, and spices, including salt. Do not confuse this with the "Nutrition Facts" section, which may list naturally occurring sugar. For example, the label on a can of tomato paste may list tomatoes as the only ingredient and yet under the "Nutrition Facts" section it may list 3 grams of sugar. The 3 grams of sugar naturally occur in the tomatoes. Check all labels regularly as manufacturers often alter ingredients.

3. It is absolutely necessary to read all labels. Low calorie, lite, light, sugarless or sugar-free on a product label does not imply that the manufacturer has not added sugar in one of its many other forms.

4. Fresh is best. If fresh fruit is not available, use frozen fruit or canned fruit packed in water or in its own juice. If juice is used, include it as part of the measurement.

5

WHEN IN DOUBT, LEAVE IT OUT!

5. Never use cornstarch or other thickeners.

6. For those with elevated cholesterol levels, limit eggs and red meats to three times a week. This meal plan may help alleviate elevated triglycerides and elevated cholesterol levels caused by excessive carbohydrates and fats.

7. Red meat should be limited to three to five times per week. Other sources of protein include tofu, tempeh, beans, chicken, fish, low-fat ricotta and low-fat cottage cheese.

8. If constipation is a problem, eight 8-oz. glasses of water per day added to your meal plan will help. Exercise, even walking, will also help. Two teaspoons of ground flaxseed on your cereal is also useful.

9. Tomato juice or vegetable cocktail juice without sugar may be used as a cooked vegetable substitute. 1 cup juice = 1 cup cooked vegetables.

10. Caffeine is an addictive stimulant and should be avoided. Suggested drinks are decaffeinated coffee, decaffeinated tea, herbal tea, carbonated water, and water.

11. Two or more proteins may be combined to equal one protein serving. For example, two ounces of cooked ground meat and one-half cup of pinto beans equals four ounces of protein.

12. For abstainers with high blood pressure who are prescribed a low sodium diet, fresh is best, frozen is the next best. Always read the label for sodium content as well as sugar. "Instant" anything has a higher sodium content.

13. You may use part of your milk allowance as a coffee lightener. One percent or skim milk may be used in this plan.

14. Do not use "sugar-free" substitutes. These have been found to create the same cravings and weight gain as refined sugars.

PRIOR PLANNING PREVENTS POOR PERFORMANCE.
IF YOU FAIL TO PLAN, THEN YOU HAVE PLANNED TO FAIL.

SUGGESTIONS FOR IMPLEMENTING ABSTINENCE

1. Following the FAA food plan as written will allow you to become well physically, mentally, and spiritually. The FAA food plan balances proteins and carbohydrates to support steady, stable blood sugar levels and a steady metabolism-essential to prevent triggering cravings and binges. The recommended time between meals further supports this. **DO NOT SKIP MEALS!** This schedule works best:

Breakfast + 4 hours = Lunch + 5 hours = Dinner + 4 hours = Metabolic Adjustment

2. Active participation in the fellowship through service is one of the best ways to help keep your commitment to recovery.

3. Have your doctor review this program of eating and follow his/her suggestions.

4. Your food should be written down. By writing your menu for a week, shopping is easier. Planning helps eliminate chaos and last minute choices made when hungry. Going over your meal plan with your sponsor daily will help you feel comfortable at planning nutritious and interesting meals and will affirm your commitment to remain abstinent. A daily log of everything you eat is an additional reinforcement.

5. DO NOT WEIGH YOURSELF more than once a month. If you are over or under your ideal weight, you may expect to lose or gain weight on this plan safely and appropriately.

6. If something listed on this food program is or becomes a problem for you, eliminate it.

7. SIT DOWN FOR MEALS AND EAT SLOWLY.

8. Include fish or poultry in your food plan daily if possible.

9. We suggest one vegetarian day per week. Try soy protein (tofu or tempeh). Check meat substitutes for wheat.

10. Beware of products advertised as low-calorie, low-fat, or fat-free. They frequently contain sugar or flour in some form.

11. When eating in a restaurant, ask questions. It's OK to ask for what you need!

12. We suggest taking a multi-vitamin daily. Check vitamins for sugar, flour and wheat. Ask the doctor or pharmacist to recommend medications that are free of sugar, alcohol, flour, and wheat whenever possible.

7

13. Do not repeat the use of any starchy vegetable or grain more than THREE times per week. We can become sensitive with overuse.

14. The following food plan is a way of eating that is free of sugar, wheat, and flour. The food plan eliminates the basic components of our binge foods: sugar, flour, wheat and inordinate amounts of fat (sticky, greasy, pasty foods). This is not a reducing diet because it is not severely restricted in terms of basic food groups. However, it does reduce fat intake to an appropriate level.

THE FAA FOOD PLAN

BREAKFAST	LUNCH	DINNER	METABOLIC ADJUSTMENT
1 protein	1 protein	1 protein	1 fruit
1 Fruit	1 cup salad or raw vegetable	1 cup salad or raw vegetable	1 dairy or 2 oz. protein
1 Dairy	1 cup cooked vegetable	1 cup cooked vegetable	
1 grain (or starchy vegetable)	Men: Add 1 fruit, 1 grain (or starchy vegetable)	1 grain (or starchy vegetable)	

The daily requirement for oil is one serving for women and two servings for men, to be divided among two or three meals.

Men need to add two ounces of fish or poultry or one ounce of red meat at each meal to the amounts shown on the list. At lunch, also add a serving of one of the following: a fruit, a grain or a starchy vegetable.

This food plan is designed for adults. For children who need to address food addiction, we recommend that your pediatrician evaluate this food plan to determine your child's needs.

Clear soup is permitted before lunch OR dinner.

NOTE: Because of our carbohydrate sensitivity, we totally eliminate all artifical sweeteners. We have found that all sweeteners can be abused like sugar, and create the same cravings and weight gain.

ROTATE ALL FOODS.
WEIGH AND MEASURE ALL FOODS.
WRITE, COMMIT, AND FOLLOW YOUR PLAN AS SPECIFIED.
WHEN IN DOUBT, LEAVE IT OUT.

This food plan is designed to allow you to live in the real world. We learn how to eat to live instead of living to eat. We can fill our emotional needs from sources other than food.

COOKED PROTEIN	SERVING SIZE	STARCHY VEGETABLES	SERVING SIZE
beef	4 ounces	all dried beans:	1/2 c.
chicken	4 ounces	lima, pinto,navy,	cooked
veal	4 ounces	corn: kernel,	1/2 c.
pork	4 ounces	corn: ear	1 med.
lamb	4 ounces	parsnips	1/2 c.
turkey	4 ounces	peas, dried	1/2 c. cooked
shellfish	4 ounces	peas, green	1/2 c.
fish	4 ounces	potato: sweet(cooked)	1 small, 6 oz.
hot dogs(not sugar cured)	4 ounces	white (baked)	1 small, 6 oz.
eggs	2 medium	mashed yams	1/2 c.
		white mashed	1/2 c.
vegetarian protein (tofu, tempeh	6 ounces	pumpkin	1/2 c.
		squash: winter, acorn, Hubbard, butternut,	
dried beans)	1 c. cooked	spaghetti, etc.	1/2 c.

9

VEGETABLES		FRUIT	SERVING
1 cup of any of the following:		apple	4" dia.
artichoke	mushrooms	apple juice	1/2 c.
asparagus	okra	applesauce	1/2 c.
bamboo shoots	onions	citrus juice	1 c.
beans: yellow	peppers: green	apricots	3 medium
green	red or yellow	all berries,	1 c.
beets	pimentos	cantaloupe	1/2 (6")
bok choy	radishes	cherries	1 c.
broccoli	rhubarb	cranberry juice	1 c.
brussel sprouts	romaine	fruit cocktail	1 c.
cabbage	rutabaga	grapefruit	1/2 large
carrots	sauerkraut	grapes	1 c.
cauliflower	snow pea pods	honeydew	1/4 (7")
celery	spinach	kiwi	3 small
chicory	summer squash	lemons, limes	2 sm/1 lg.
chinese cabbage	swiss chard	nectarines	2 sm/1 lg
Cucumber	tomatoes	orange	1 med.
eggplant	turnips	peach	1 large
endive	vegetable juice	pear	1 large
escarole	watercress	pineapple	1 c.
greens: beet,	zucchini	pineapple juice	1/2 c.
dandelion, kale	any sprouts,	plums	3 medium
mustard,turnip, collard		prune juice	1/2 c.
all types of lettuce		tangerine	2 small
dill pickles		watermelon	1 c.

GRAINS

1 cup of any of the following, measured after cooking:

amaranth	barley
brown rice	buckwheat
cream of rye	grits
millet	oat bran (1/2 c. raw = 1 c. cooked)
oatmeal	quinoa
rye	

1 cup of any non-wheat, sugar-free, dry cereal such as:

puffed brown rice	puffed millet
puffed corn	3 rice cakes = 1 serving

DAIRY (May also be used as a protein.)

buttermilk	1 cup	low fat cottage cheese	½ cup
low fat ricotta cheese	½ cup	low fat yogurt	1 cup
milk: skim or 1%	1 cup	soy beverage	1 cup

If you are dairy sensitive, eliminate dairy and substitute 2 oz. of any type of protein.

FATS

Polyunsaturated oils are essential to good health. Women require one fat serving per day and men require two. The fat requirement is normally divided between two or more meals. Choose from the following:

oil - 1 tablespoon,	margarine - 1 tablespoon
mayonnaise - 1 tablespoon	salad dressing - 2 tablespoons

CONDIMENTS

Any sugar-free, alcohol-free, wheat-free spice or sauce including but not limited to mustard, tamari, salsa, non-fat yogurt, lemon juice, etc. Limit spice and condiment use to the levels recommended in recipes or no more than 1 teaspoon per day of any one spice and no more than two tablespoons per day of any one sauce.

This initial food plan has been the most successful for our members to obtain abstinence, enabling them to begin to have clear thinking. Eating the prescribed food plan also offers us a chance to heal our organs and learn the basic fundamentals of healthy eating. To maintain abstinence, an open mind will be required while our bodies heal and our needs change. The most important aspect of maintaining abstinence is to totally eliminate sugar, flour and wheat from our daily lives.

Most food addicts do achieve and maintain a healthy weight by following this plan. Nonetheless, we would like to address the question of what to do when a person following the food plan continues to lose weight after reaching a healthy weight or when a person who is underweight when they begin the program fails to gain. This guide is intended to focus on recovery for food addicts as a whole rather than to address specific situations that arise in recovery. Although unusual, if weight loss or failure to gain continues over time to an inappropriate level, any changes needed to stabilize one's weight should be developed with the assistance of a sponsor, physician or other qualified professional. The most important thing is to maintain close contact with one's sponsor and remain totally honest about what we are eating, how much we weigh, how our bodies are functioning, and how we are feeling physically.

HOW TO BEGIN...
A list of supplies you will need to begin cooking

PANS WITH LIDS

1 Qt., 2 Qt., 3 Qt., 6 Qt., Dutch Oven, Saute, Omelette & Flat Skillets, Griddle and Wok.

Enameled Roasting Pan, self basting, Broiler Pan, 2 Qt. and 4 Qt. Glass Baking Dishes with Lids

COOKING UTENSILS
Set of Nested Measuring Cups, Glass Measuring Cup for measuring liquids, Measuring Spoons, Scale that weighs up to 1 lb.(treat yourself to a digital scale,) Plastic Bowls w/Lids for storing unused portions, Blender, Mixer, Food Processor, Funnel, Whisk, Wooden Spoons, Slotted Spoon, Spatula, Grater, Baster, Steamer, Sharp Kitchen Knives, Garlic Press, Sieve, Strainer, Vegetable Peeler

Buy the best, waterless stainless steel cookware you can afford. It is a lifetime investment that will be used everyday and offers an opportunity to get the nourishment from the food we eat for a healthy body. Learn to use the Time/Bake feature on your oven range, it saves time and is energy conscious. Put similar in size, either all frozen or thawed, turkey breast or whole roasting chicken, beef or pork roast in a self-basting enamel roaster, set the oven at 250°. Use the time-bake feature on the oven to bake in the middle of the night and turn off by morning. When you arise, you will have a warm protein serving for breakfast. This can be portioned, then stored in the refrigerator for later use.

13

SPICES AND SEASONINGS

Allspice   Anise Seed

Basil   Bay leaf   Black Pepper

Cajun seasoning   Cayenne Pepper   Celery Seed   Chili Powder   Chinese Five Spice   Chive   Cilantro   Cinnamon   Cloves   Cumin   Curry

Dill   Dry Mustard   Fennel Seed   Garlic Powder   Garlic Salt   Ginger Marjoram   Mint   Nutmeg   Oregano   Paprika   Parsley   Poultry Seasoning Rosemary   Saffron   Sage   Spike   Tarragon   Thyme   Turmeric Wheat/Alcohol Free Tamari   Bottled Lemon Juice   Bottled Hot Sauce

Non-Stick Spray for pans.

Some of these can be grown easily at home:
Basil   Cilantro   Dill   Garlic   Mint   Parsley

WARNING!!!!!!!

Even if the recipe does not specifically state it, all ingredients in each and every recipe must be sugar, flour and wheat free.

SUBSTITUTIONS

When using a recipe from another source, remember you can often substitute oatmeal/oat bran/cream of rye for bread or cracker crumbs, applesauce or mashed pears/peaches/crushed pineapple for honey or syrup. Meat substitute products frequently contain wheat. Check labels carefully.

NAMES OF SUGAR, FLOUR & WHEAT

Types & forms of sugar
Ace-K
Acesulfame-k (Sunette, Sweet and Safe, Sweet One)
Alcohol, alcoholic drinks
Alitame
Amasake
Artificial Sweetners-All artificial sweeteners are considered sugar in FAA
Artificial sweetener packets (Equal, Sweet'n'low, Sweet Thing, Splenda)
Artificial flavors (check with company)
Aspartame/NutraSweet
Augmiel
Barley malt
Cane juice
Caramel coloring
Concentrated fruit juice
Corn sweetener
Cyclamates
Date paste, syrup
Dextrin
Dried/dehydrated fruit
Evaporated cane juice (e.g., Florida Crystals)
Extracts
Fat substitutes (made from concentrated fruit paste)
Fructooligosaccharides (FOS)
Fruit flavorings (check with company)
Fruit juice concentrate
Glucoamine/glucosamine
Glycerine
Honey (any type)
Jaggery
-ides, any additive with this suffix:
monosodium glycerides, olyglycerides, saccharides (any), trisaccharides, diglycerides, disaccharides, glycerides (any), monoglycerides, onosaccharides, etc.
Licorice root powder
"Light", "lite" or "low" sugar
Malted barley

Types & forms of sugar (continued)

Maltodextrins
Malts (any)
Molasses, black strap molasses
"Natural" flavors (call company)
"Natural" sweeteners
Nectars
Neotame
-ol, any additive with this suffix:
carbitol, glucitol, glycerol, glycol, hexitol, inversol, maltitol, mannitol, sorbitol, xylitol, etc.
Olestra (made from sucrose)
-ose, these additives with this suffix:
colorose, dextrose, fructose, galactose, glucose, lactose, levulose, maltodextrose, maltose, mannose, polydextrose, polytose, ribose, sucralose, sucrose, tagatose, zylose.
Raisin juice, pastc or syrup
Rice malt, sugar or syrup
Rice sweeteners
Sorghum
Splenda (Sucralose)
Stevia
Sucanat (evaporated cane juice)
Sucraryl
Sugars, any type:
apple sugar, barbados sugar, bark sugar, beet sugar, brown sugar (any grade), cane sugar, caramel sugars, confectioner's sugar, date sugar, grape sugar, invert sugar, milled sugar, "natural" sugar, powdered sugar, raw sugar, turbinado sugar, unrefined sugar, etc.
Sunenette/Sweet-One (Acesulfame-K)
Syrups, any type:
agave syrup, barley syrup, brown rice syrup, corn syrup, date syrup, high fructose corn syrup, maple syrup, raisin syrup, yinnie syrup (rice syrup), etc.
Vanillan
Whey (as an additive)
Xanthum gum
REMEMBER: All types of artificial sweeteners are considered sugar in FAA

Types & forms of flour

Any bean, vegetable, nut, or grain that is ground into flour, meal, or powder is "flour," as the term is used in the FAA Definition of Abstinence.
Starches and guar gum are also considered flour.

We do not consume any kind of flour.

Types & forms of wheat
Bran (if made from wheat)
Bulgar
Cracked wheat
Durum wheat
Gluten (wheat protein)
Kamut
Red wheat
Red spring wheat
Seitan (made from wheat protein, gluten)
Semolina
Spelt
Triticale (a wheat/rye hybrid)
Wheat berries
Wheat bran
Wheat flakes
Wheat germ
Whole-grain wheat
Winter wheat

Please note:
This list is not exhaustive. If you are unsure about an ingredient, it is best to check with the manufacturer or forego the product.

To lessen your confusion remember:
Fresh is best. Minimal use of processed foods is the simplest way to avoid additives containing sugar, flour or wheat.

ADDITIONAL RECIPES

CONDIMENTS

WARNING!!!!!

Even if the recipe does not specifically state it, all ingredients in each and every recipe must be sugar, flour and wheat free.

Condiments

GARBANZO SPREAD

1/2 Red Onion, chopped
1 1/2 Tbls. Oil
1/2 bunch Parsley, chopped fine
Salt to taste
1 tsp. Basil
1/2 tsp. Oregano
1/4 tsp. Cumin and Garlic Powder (Best: 2 cloves fresh garlic)
Small Lemon, juice only
3 C. Garbanzo Beans, cooked, mashed

Blend all ingredients together, use 1 cup as protein spread on rice cake. Stuff a ripe tomato and it becomes a protein with a vegetable. Garbanzo Spread can be used as salad dressing by thinning with water until desired consistency. This spread does not need refrigeration and can be used for traveling or camping, hiking, etc. Try one of the Salsa recipes over this spread.

1 cup = 1 protein, 1/2 Tbl oil

TOMATO-TARRAGON TOPPING

1 tsp. Olive Oil
1/2 C. Onion, finely chopped
1/4 C. Celery, finely chopped
1-1/2 C. Tomato, diced & seeded
1-1/2 tsp.Tarragon, fresh, chopped
1/4 tsp. Salt
1/8 tsp. Pepper
1 Tbls. Lemon Juice, fresh

Heat oil in a large non stick skillet over high heat. Add onion and celery; saute 1 minute. Add tomato; saute 1-1/2 minutes or until tender. Remove from heat; stir in Tarragon and remaining ingredients. Serve over Halibut or Cod.

1/4 cup on each seafood serving = 1/4 cup cooked vegetable.

19

DIJON SAUCE

2 tsp. Dijon Mustard
1 Garlic Clove, crushed
1 Tbls. Water
2 tsp. Lemon Juice
Mix together and chill.

2 Tablespoons = 1 serving sauce

FENNEL-LEEK TOPPING

1 tsp. Olive Oil
2/3 C. Coarsely chopped Fennel Bulb (about 1 large)
1 C. Leeks, sliced (about 1 medium)
2/3 C. Water
2 Tbls. Chopped Fennel Leaves
1/4 tsp. Salt
1/8 tsp. Pepper

Heat oil in a large non stick skillet over medium-high heat. Add fennel bulb and leek; saute 5 minutes. Add water; Cover and cook 20 minutes. Uncover; Cook 7 minutes or until moisture evaporates, stirring occasionally. Remove from heat; stir in remaining ingredients.

Serve 1/4 cup over salmon = 1/4 cup cooked vegetable.

GINGER SAUCE

3 Ginger Root (1/2 inch) cubes, peeled, chopped
1/2 C. Wheat/Alcohol Free Tamari
1/4 C. Vinegar
1 large Onion

Place ginger, Tamari, vinegar and onion in blender container. Blend on high speed for 2 minutes or until ginger and onion are mixed. Yield: about 3/4 cup

2 Tablespoons = 1 serving sauce

WHITE DRESSING

2 C. Low fat Buttermilk
1 C. Low fat Cottage Cheese
1/2 C. Mayonnaise
1 tsp. White Pepper
2 Tbls. Garlic
1 tsp. Salt

Process buttermilk and cottage cheese in blender until smooth. Add mayonnaise and seasonings. Process until well blended

2 Tablespoons = 1 serving salad dressing

ROASTED PEPPER TOPPING

2 Tbls. Lemon Juice, fresh
1 tsp. Extra-Virgin Olive Oil
1/2 tsp. Anchovy Paste
1/4 tsp. Pepper
1/8 tsp. Salt
1 Large Garlic Clove, crushed
1 Large Red Bell Pepper (about 1/2 pound)
1 Large Green Bell Pepper (about 1/2 pound)
1 Large Yellow Bell Pepper (about 1/2 pound)

Combine first 6 ingredients in a bowl; stir well with a wire whisk. Cover and let stand 30 minutes to 1 hour. Cut bell peppers in half lengthwise; discard seeds and membranes. Place peppers, skin side up, on a foil-lined baking sheet; flatten with palm of hand. Broil 3 inches from heat for 12 minutes or until blackened and charred. Place peppers in a zip-lock bag and seal; let stand 15 minutes. Peel and discard skins. Cut roasted bell peppers lengthwise into strips. Add pepper strips to lemon juice mixture; toss to coat. Cover and marinate at room temperature for 1 hour. Serve 1/4 cup over Mahi Mahi, Swordfish, Halibut, Red Snapper or Grouper.

1/4 cup = 1/4 cup cooked vegetable.

GARLICKY SPINACH TOPPING

1 tsp. Olive Oil
1/2 C. Onion, finely chopped
3 Large Cloves Garlic, minced
2 Tbls. Balsamic Vinegar
1/3 C. Water
8 C. Spinach (about 3/4 lb.), tightly packed, torn, fresh
1/4 tsp. Salt
1/8 tsp. Pepper
Dash of Nutmeg

Heat oil in a large non stick skillet over medium heat. Add onion and garlic; saute 3 minutes. Add vinegar; Cook 30 seconds or until liquid evaporates, stirring constantly. Add water and cook 4 minutes or until reduced by half. Add spinach and next 3 ingredients. Cook 3 minutes or until spinach wilts, stirring constantly.

Serve 1/4 C. over salmon = 1/4 C. cooked vegetable

MAYONNAISE

One Egg Yolk
1 C. Vegetable or Safflower Oil
2 tsp. Lemon Juice

Beat the egg yolk in a mixing bowl, adding the oil a teaspoon at a time until it begins to thicken. Add lemon Juice to thin the mixture to suit your taste. If it gets too thin, add more oil. This Mayonnaise is low in cholesterol, doesn't contain preservatives and other chemicals and is sugar free. Prepared mayonnaise often contains sugar and a high degree of cholesterol, unless fat free is used which usually contains sugar. When making any salad add 1/2 yogurt and 1/2 mayonnaise and lower the fat content of your meal.

BARBECUE SAUCE

1/2 C. (no-sugar) Salsa, mild or medium
1 tsp. Wheat/Alcohol Free Tamari
1/2 tsp. Vinegar or Lemon Juice
1/4-1/2 tsp.(to taste) Liquid Hickory Smoke
Herbs and Spices to taste

Heat Salsa and vinegar or lemon juice together. Add desired herbs and spices. Remove from heat. Add liquid smoke and stir. Yield: about 1/2 Cup.

2 Tablespoons = 1 serving sauce

ALMOST CATSUP

1 C. Tomato Sauce
1/2 tsp. Dry Mustard
1 tsp. Vinegar
Dash Black Pepper
1/2 tsp. Garlic Powder
1 tsp. Wheat/Alcohol Free Tamari

Bring ingredients to boil stirring constantly, simmer over very low heat for 10 min. Cool before serving.

2 Tablespoons = 1 serving sauce

FRENCH DRESSING

1 C. Homemade Mayonnaise
1/4 C. Homemade Catsup
1 Tbls. Vinegar or Lemon Juice
Store in refrigerator until needed.

Use 1 Tablespoon. for each cup of Salad.

23

LEMON HERB VINAIGRETTE

In a small bowl, combine 1/2 C. Olive Oil, 1/4 C. Balsamic Vinegar, 1/4 C. Fresh Lemon Juice, 2 Tbls. finely chopped Lemon Zest, 1 minced Garlic Clove, 1 Tbls. Fresh (or 1 tsp. dried) Tarragon. Salt and Pepper to taste; whisk thoroughly. Yield: 1 Cup

2 Tablespoons= 1 serving salad dressing

ZERO SALAD DRESSING

1 Onion, medium
2 C. Tomato or V 8 Juice
1/2 C. Lemon Juice
Salt, Pepper, Garlic, Parsley to taste

Peel onion and cut into pieces. Process in blender with 1 C. tomato juice until smooth. Add remaining tomato juice and lemon juice. Process until well blended. Stir in seasonings to taste. Yield: 2-1/2 Cups

2 Tablespoons= 1 serving salad dressing

ITALIAN DRESSING

7 oz. Olive Oil
1/2 C. Balsamic Vinegar
1 tsp. Garlic, chopped or 1/2 tsp.Garlic Powder
1 tsp. Basil
1 tsp. Oregano
2 tsp. Wheat/Alcohol Free Tamari

Store in cupboard, not refrigerator (oil separates). Make in advance so spices have time to blend.

2 Tablespoons= 1 serving salad dressing

YOGURT-DILL DRESSING

1 8 oz. carton Plain Non-fat Yogurt
2 tsp. Onion, finely chopped
1/2 tsp. Dill Weed, crushed
1/4 tsp. Dry Mustard
1/2 tsp. Garlic Powder

Mix all ingredients. Chill well. Serve over sliced tomatoes. This can also be used as a marinade for chicken or fish before broiling or grilling

LOW-FAT DRESSING

8 oz. Tofu
1 C. Non-fat Yogurt
1/4 C. Vinegar, Balsamic Vinegar or Lemon Juice
Balsamic is preferable
2 fresh Garlic Cloves
Sprinkle Black Pepper
2 Tbls. Wheat/Alcohol Free Tamari
Several Sprigs of Fresh Parsley
1 Tomato
1/2 Green Pepper
1/2 Peeled Cucumber
Onion, Basil and Oregano can be added if desired.

Put all ingredients into blender on low speed. Blend until all vegetables are pureed and mixture is smooth. Store in glass jar in refrigerator for up to two weeks. Use as salad dressing or as an marinade on chicken or fish before grilling.

2 Tablespoons= 1 serving salad dressing

25

COTTAGE CHEESE SPREAD

1 C. Low-Fat Cottage Cheese
1/4 C. Radishes, chopped small
1/2 tsp. Lemon Rind, grated
1 Clove Garlic, chopped
2 Tbls. Fresh Basil, chopped or 1 Tbl. dry
1/4 C. Fresh Carrot, grated

Blend cottage cheese in blender or food processor until smooth. Spoon into a small bowl, and add in the remaining ingredients. Mix; chill for 2 hrs.
3/4 C. = 1/2 C. cottage cheese and 1/4 C. raw vegetable.

CORN SALSA

2 Ears Corn (remove kernels from cob), diced fine
3/4 C. Yellow Pepper (or Red)
3/4 C. Yellow or Cherry Tomatoes
1/4 C. Scallion, white part only
1 Tbls. Cilantro

Mix ingredients together and let stand for 1 hour for flavor to blend. Makes 2 servings. 1/2 recipe=
1 starchy vegetable and 3/4 cup raw vegetable each serving.
(Note: You could add 1/4 C. carrots to complete the vegetable portion)

SALSA

3 Medium Ripe Tomatoes, chopped
1/2 Onion, large
Small bunch of fresh Cilantro, chopped very fine
1/2 tsp. Salt
1 Tbls. Olive Oil

Mix all ingredients together and chill 2 hours before serving.
1/2 cup = 1/2 cup raw vegetable

ZINGY SALSA

1 Tomato, large, ripe, remove seeds
1 Onion, small
2 Tbls. Cilantro
1 Jalapeno Pepper
1/2 C. Lime Juice

Chop all ingredients very fine or use a food processor;
1/2 cup = 1/2 cup raw vegetable.

HUMUS AND VEGETABLES

2 C. Garbanzo beans (chick peas)
1 Tbls. + 1 Tsp Olive Oil
1 tsp.Tahini
1 Clove Garlic
1 tsp. Lemon Juice
Assorted chilled vegetables

Combine first 5 ingredients in food processor. Blend on high for 30 seconds. Stir and blend for 30 seconds more. Serve with assorted, cold, chopped Vegetables.
1 cup humus = 1 protein, 2 tsp. oil

ADDITIONAL RECIPES

BREAKFAST

WARNING!!!!!

Even if the recipe does not specifically state it, all ingredients in each and every recipe must be sugar, flour and wheat free.

Breakfast

BREAKFAST SOUFFLE

4 Egg Whites, slightly beaten
1/2 C. Oatmeal or 1/3 C. of Cream of Rye or Quinoa Flakes
1/2 C. Applesauce

Spray bowl with non stick spray. Place all ingredients in bowl, mix well and microwave, covered, for 2 minutes. Yield: one serving
1 recipe= 1 protein, 1 grain, 1 fruit

QUINOA CEREAL

1 C. Water
1/3 C. Quinoa Cereal
1 C. Crushed Pineapple, drained
or other fruit.
Cook Quinoa in water until water is obsorbed. Fold in Pineapple or other fruit and serve.
Serving = 1 fruit, 1 grain

BAKED OATMEAL WITH APPLE

2 C. Skim milk or unsweetened soy milk
1 Tbl. Ground cinnamon
8 whole eggs or 1 C. Egg whites
4 C. Uncooked oatmeal
4 C. Diced peeled apples
Preheat oven 350° F. In a large bowl, combine milk and cinnamon. In another bowl, beat egg whites or whole eggs until frothy, add to milk mixture and stir to combine thoroughly. Add oatmeal and toss well.

Fold in diced apples and pour into a non-stick or lightly oiled 8x12x2 inch baking dish. Bake 45 to 50 minutes. Serve cold, room temperature, or warm with milk. Freezes well. Delicious! Yield: 8 servings.

1/8 recipe= 1 grain, 3/4 protein, 1/2 fruit each.
(Note: to complete the breakfast, you could add 1 1/4 cup skim milk, 1/2 fruit)

OATMEAL DELIGHT

Breakfast

2 Eggs
1/2 C. Low fat Cottage Cheese
1/2 C. Raw Oatmeal, or half Oatmeal and half Oat Bran or Cream of Rye
1/8 tsp. Salt

Place all ingredients in blender or food processor and blend 5-6 seconds.
Drop by tablespoons onto hot griddle that has been sprayed with vegetable
spray. Turn over when bubbles appear on surface and cook 1 more minute.
Serve with fresh berries or fruit.

Yield:1 Serving = 1 protein,1 dairy, 1 grain

BREAKFAST PATTIE

4 Egg Whites
1 Apple or other firm fruit
1/4 C. Raw Old Fashion Oatmeal
1/2 Serving of any other grain (it can either be cooked or raw)

Mix all ingredients together. Form two patties on griddle and cook, turning
once. Excellent non-dairy breakfast. Freezes well. Yield 1 Serving

1 Serving = 1 protein, 1 grain, 1 fruit

VEGETARIAN DISHES

WARNING!!!!!

Even if the recipe does not specifically state it, all ingredients in each and every recipe must be sugar, flour and wheat free.

EGGPLANT

2 Small Eggplant
2 C. Low-Fat Skim Milk Ricotta Cheese
1 C. Crushed Tomatoes
1 tsp. Basil
1 tsp. Oregano,
1/2 tsp. Anise Seed
1 C. Onions, sauteed

Peel eggplants (the smaller eggplant are more tender), slice thin and soak in salt water for 10-15 minutes to remove bitterness. Rinse well. Place in layers in baking dish; eggplant, crumbled ricotta cheese. Add basil, oregano and anise to crushed tomatoes and sauteed onions. Bake at 350°, 45 minutes.
Serving size: 1-1/2 C. = 1 cooked vegetable, 4 oz. protein

BLACK-EYED PEAS & RICE

1 lb. Dried Peas
1 C. Brown Basmati rice or brown rice
Soak peas overnight in salted water. Drain and rinse. Cook until tender with carrots, onions, celery, bay leaf & 2 Tbls. Tamari. Cook rice in 2 cups water until done. Spoon 1/2 C. peas over 1 C. cooked rice for each serving.
1 Serving = 1 protein, 1 grain

TOFU WITH PESTO AND TOMATO SAUCE

16 oz. Tofu
16 oz. Prepared Marinara Sauce or Crushed Tomatoes
1 Container of Prepared Pesto. Add:
1 Tbl. Fresh Basil
1 Tbl. Fresh Garlic
Blend well with Pesto. Slice tofu, brown on both sides with non stick spray. Layer 6 oz. Tofu in pan with 1 cup Pesto and tomato sauce ending with tomato sauce. Bake 25 min. at 350°
6 ounces Tofu = 1 protein, 1 C. sauce = 1 cooked vegetable

31

BLACK BEANS AND CORN

1 Green Pepper, chopped
1 (16 oz) frozen Corn, cook and drain well
1 (16 oz.) Can Black Beans, well drained
1/8 C. Olive Oil
1 small Onion, chopped fine
2 Plum Tomatoes, seeded and chopped
1 tsp. Curry Powder
1/8 tsp. Red Pepper (Cayenne)
1 Garlic Clove, minced

Combine all ingredients; mix well. Cover and refrigerate 3 to 4 hours
Serve hot or cold
1 1/4 C. = 1/2 cup starchy vegetable, 1/4 C. raw vegetable and 4oz. protein.

VEGETARIAN ITALIAN DISH

1/2 C. Low-Fat Ricotta Cheese
1/2 C. Tomatoes, chopped
1/4 C. Bell Peppers, chopped
1/4 C. Onion, chopped
1 Garlic Clove
1/2 Tbl. Olive Oil
Salt, Pepper, Basil
1 C. Quinoa, cooked

Saute vegetables in 1/2 tablespoon oil. Stir in Ricotta Cheese. Season to taste. Serve over Quinoa with green salad.
Yield 1 serving
1 Serving = 1 protein, 1 grain, 1 cup cooked vegetable, 1/2 Tbl. oil.

LENTIL AND VEGETABLE SALAD
WITH GARLICKY GINGER DRESSING

2 Tbls. Cider Vinegar

2 tsps. Dijon-style Mustard

1 or 2 Cloves Garlic, crushed

1 tsp. Ground Ginger

1/4 tsp. Salt

1/4 C. Water

1 Tbls. Olive Oil

1 C. Dry Lentils, picked over and rinsed

2 C. Water

1/4 tsp. Salt

1/2 lb. Green Beans, trim ends

Soft Lettuce Leaves

2 Ripe Plum Tomatoes, cut into long wedges

1/2 C. Sweet Yellow or Orange Pepper, finely chopped

Prepare dressing: Whisk together vinegar, mustard, garlic, ginger and salt in medium bowl. Slowly whisk in the 1/4 C. water; and the oil until blended. Prepare salad: Combine lentils, 2 C. water, salt in medium-size sauce pan. Bring to boil over medium heat. Lower heat; Simmer partially covered, 20 minutes, until lentils are soft but still shapely. Meanwhile, steam the green beans over boiling water for about 3 minutes; until tender-crisp. Drain well; Arrange beans on salad plates with lettuce and tomatoes; drizzle each serving with 2 teaspoons of the reserved dressing. Drain lentils. Add to bowl with remaining dressing. Add yellow pepper; toss well. Mound dressed lentils on salad plates with vegetables. Serve warm.

1/2 cup lentils = 1 starchy vegetable or 1 cup lentils = 1 protein
1 cup vegetables = 1/2 raw vegetable, 1/2 cooked vegetable
2 teaspoons dressing

FALAFEL

1 Medium Potato
1 Bunch Parsley, minced fine
2 Small Onions, chopped fine
2 Tbls. Oil
3 C. Ground cooked Garbanzo Beans, (can use canned Garbanzo Beans)
2 Green Onions, chopped, including tops.
1 Tbl. Yogurt
1/4 tsp. Garlic Powder
2 tsps. Salt
2 Dashes Cayenne Pepper
Sprinkle Black Pepper
1/4 tsp. Paprika

Vegetarian Dishes

Preheat oven to 350°. Cook and mash potato. Mince leaves of parsley, chop onions fine and saute in oil. Stir in green onion and parsley and cook briefly. Add to ground beans. Mix well with other ingredients. Form into balls using 2 tablespoons of the mixture for each one. Place on greased baking sheets and bake for 10 minutes on each side.

Serve with any one or all of the following, and count as your vegetable, oil etc.: Any Salsa recipe. Shredded lettuce, diced tomato, diced green pepper, diced cucumber, shredded mushrooms, yogurt, dash of oil and vinegar. This travels well. Does not need refrigeration.

3 Falafels = 1 starchy vegetable

BROCCOLI AND BROWN RICE SALAD

2-1/2 C. Chicken or Vegetable Broth
1 C. Brown Rice
1 Medium Bunch Broccoli, cut in flowerets and stems peeled and sliced crosswise

1 Carrot, thinly sliced with vegetable peeler
1 Sweet Red Pepper, cored, seeded and diced
6 Green Onions, finely chopped
Lemon-Herb Vinaigrette
1/4 C. Fresh Parsley, chopped
6 Large Radishes with leaves

In medium saucepan, bring broth to a boil; add rice and cover. Lower heat and simmer 50 minutes or until liquid has absorbed. Transfer rice to a bowl and chill 1 hour.

Meanwhile, in a large saucepan of boiling water blanch broccoli 3 to 5 minutes or until crisp-tender. Drain and rinse with cold water.

Combine broccoli, carrot, red pepper and green onions. Toss 1 cup vegetables with 1 cup rice and 1 1/2 tsp. Lemon-Herb Vinaigrette (see Condiments); cover and chill 1 hour. Before serving, add 1 Tbls. dressing and garnish with chopped parsley and radishes. Yield 4-6 servings.

1 grain, 1 cup raw vegetable, 1 Tbl. dressing

TOFU SALAD - KRISHNA

12 oz. Soft Tofu, slightly mashed
2 C. Celery, Green Pepper, Cabbage, chopped, mix well
2 tsp. Sesame Oil
Mustard (optional)
Curry Powder(optional)
Spike (optional)

Mix all ingredients together.

1/2 recipe = 6 ounces = 1 protein, 1 cup raw vegetable, 2 tsp. oil.

VEGETABLE LOAF

Vegetarian
Dishes

1 Large Eggplant
2 Medium Onions, chopped
1/2 C. Oatmeal
1 C. Scallions, chopped
1 Egg, beaten
1 tsp. Oregano
1/2 tsp. Salt
4 Tbls. Oat Bran
2 Tbls. Margarine
1/2 Bunch of Parsley, chopped
2 Tomatoes, diced
1/2 C. Green Pepper, chopped
1 Garlic Clove, minced
1 C. Celery, diced

Heat oven to 350°. Peel and chop eggplant fine, or grind in food processor. Heat margarine in large skillet and saute eggplant, onions, parsley, tomatoes, celery, green pepper and scallions. Transfer to mixing bowl; let cool. Add egg, 1/3 C. oatmeal, oregano, oat bran, garlic powder, salt to taste. Place in a greased 8-inch square baking dish. Sprinkle with remaining oatmeal. Bake for 25 minutes.

1 cup = 1 cup cooked vegetable

SPINACH, CHEESE AND TOMATO BAKE

1/2 C. Low-Fat (1%) Cottage Cheese
1/2 C. Low-Fat (1%) Milk
1 Egg
1/4 tsp. Ground Nutmeg
1/8 tsp. Dried Mint Leaves, crumbled
1 tsp. Vegetable Oil
3/4 C. Green Onions, chopped, mostly white part

1 Large Garlic Clove, finely chopped
8 oz. Plum Tomatoes, seeded and chopped
1/8 tsp. Salt
1/8 tsp. Pepper
12 oz. Fresh Spinach, washed, drained, stemmed and coarsely chopped

Preheat oven to 375°. Combine cottage cheese, milk, egg, 1/8 tsp. of the nutmeg and mint in blender. Whirl until smooth, about 1 min. Heat oil in large skillet over medium heat. Add onion; saute 2 minutes. Add garlic; saute 1 min. Add tomatoes, salt, pepper and remaining 1/8 tsp. of nutmeg; saute 2 minutes. Add spinach; stirring, until spinach is tender and liquid evaporates in 3 to 5 minutes. Pour into a 9-inch pan. Bake for 30 minutes Let stand at least 20 minutes before serving. Serve either warm or at room temperature.

1-1/2 cups = 1 cooked vegetable, 1 protein

RICE WITH CHICK PEAS

2 C. Water
1/2 tsp. Salt
1/8 tsp. Crushed Red Pepper Flakes
1 C. Brown Basmati or any Brown Rice
1 Tbls. Olive Oil
1 medium Garlic Clove, peeled and finely minced
1 medium Carrot, peeled and finely minced
1 (15-1/2- oz) Can Chick Peas (Garbanzo Beans), drained, rinsed and drained again
1 Tbls. Ginger Root, grated
3 Tbls. Lemon Juice

In a medium saucepan combine the water, salt and pepper flakes. Bring to a boil over high heat. Add the rice and bring back to a boil. Cover and cook until done. Heat olive oil in a large skillet over medium heat. Add garlic and carrots; saute 5 minutes. Add chick peas and ginger. Heat through 5 minutes. Add lemon juice and stir well. Spoon 1 C chick peas over 1 C rice.

1 C. rice = 1 protein, 1 grain, 1/2 Tbls. oil

PAT'S ABSTINENT EGGPLANT

2 C. Eggplant, sliced about 1/4 inch thick
1 C. Low Fat Ricotta Cheese
1 (8 oz.) Can Pureed Tomatoes, seasoned with:
1/4 Tbl. Garlic Powder
1/4 Tbl. Basil
1/4 Tbl. Onion Powder or Flakes

Layer eggplant and Ricotta in square glass dish and top with tomato sauce. Cook in microwave oven for 10 minutes at high heat or until tender. Serve with salad. Yield 2 Servings
1/2 recipe = 1-1/2 cup cooked vegetable, 1 protein

STUFFED PEPPERS

6 Large Green Peppers
1 C. Millet, cooked
1 C. Soft Tofu, rinsed and drained.
1 (28 oz.) Can Tomatoes crushed
3 large Shredded Carrots
1 Small Shredded Zucchini or Summer Squash
2 Tbls. Onion, chopped
4 Sprigs Fresh Parsley, chopped
1 tsp. Fennel
1/2 tsp. Anise Seed, Basil and Garlic Powder
2 Tbls. Wheat Free Tamari

Bring 2 cups water to a boil, add millet. Cover and reduce heat to lowest setting. Let cook until almost tender. Drain off any liquid. Mix cooked millet, shredded carrots, shredded zucchini or summer squash together with soft tofu, 1/2 can crushed tomatoes seasoned with fennel, anise, basil, Tamari, dried parsley, black pepper and sauteed onions. Save remaining crushed tomatoes to pour over the stuffed peppers before baking. Stuff into green peppers that have been cut in half and core discarded. Lay in baking pan. Pour remaining crushed tomato mixture over peppers. Bake at 325° for 1 hr. You could use one of the already prepared marinara sauces without sugar. For variation, add 1 lb. ground turkey or beef instead of tofu.
1 Pepper = 1 cooked vegetable, 1/6 grain, 1/6 protein (tofu), or 1/2 protein (turkey or beef.)

SEAFOOD

Seafood

WARNING!!!!!

Even if the recipe does not specifically state it, all ingredients in each and every recipe must be sugar, flour and wheat free.

HOW TO GRILL FISH

1. Heat grill
2. Rub raw, peeled potato on hot grill rack (the potato will keep the fish from sticking).
3. Place raw fish on grill (skin on top) and cook
4. Turn fish and cook until the fish flakes

Note: All baked fish recipes work well on the grill.

CHARCOAL GRILLED WHITE FISH

3 lbs. any type of White Fish (cod, haddock, flounder)
1/4 C. Oil
1/2 C. Lemon Juice
1/2 tsp. Salt
1/2 tsp. Pepper
1 Tbls. Oregano
1/4 tsp. Garlic Powder

Mix all ingredients except fish. Brush mixture over fish. Cook over coals until golden brown. Place on serving platter and pour remaining mixture over fish.

4 ounces, cooked = 1 protein, 1 Tbls. oil

SHRIMP FOO YUNG

6 Eggs
1/8 tsp. Ginger
1 C. Green Onion, chopped
8 oz. Shrimp, cooked fresh or frozen
1 C. Water Chestnuts, chopped
1 Can Bean Sprouts, drained

Beat eggs, add spices, water chestnuts, bean sprouts and shrimp. Spray wok with non-stick spray. Place egg mixture in heated wok. Loosen around cooked edges and tilt raw mixture underneath until fully cooked.

6 oz. = 1 protein, 1/2 cup cooked vegetable.

Seafood

39

FLOUNDER IN LEMON-DILL SAUCE

3 Tbls. Chicken Broth
1 Tbls. Fresh Dill, chopped or 3/4 tsp. dried
1 Tbl. Lemon Juice
1/4 tsp. Salt (optional)
1 Medium Green Onion, thinly sliced
1 lb. Flounder Fillets
Lemon slices for garnish

Purchase fresh or frozen flounder fillets. Thaw frozen flounder fillets. In a 10 inch skillet over medium-low heat, heat chicken broth and next 4 ingredients, stir occasionally, until bubbly. If flounder fillets are large, cut into serving-size pieces. Add flounder to mixture in skillet; cover and cook 5 to 8 minutes, until flounder flakes easily when tested with a fork. Arrange flounder with its sauce in warm, deep platter. Garnish with lemon slices.

4 oz. = 1 protein, 2 tablespoons sauce

ORIENTAL SWORDFISH

6 oz. Fillet of Swordfish
1 Tbls. Vinaigrette Dressing (see Condiments)
3 Tbls. Tamari

Marinate swordfish in dressing and Tamari for 2 hours before cooking. Place on baking sheet and pour any remaining marinade over fish. Broil on high for 6 minutes on each side.

4 oz. serving = 1 protein

SALMON CROQUETTES

1 Can Pink Salmon (13-1/2 oz.)
1 Egg
2 Tbls. Mayonnaise
1/3 C. Oatmeal
1/4 C. Onion, chopped
1/4 C. Green Pepper (optional)
1 Tbls. Dill Weed
2 Tbls. Olive Oil

Heat oil in skillet on low heat. Remove bones from salmon.
Mix mayonnaise, dill, egg, onion, pepper and dill weed in a separate dish.
Combine salmon with mixture and make into patties. Roll in oatmeal
until oatmeal covers most of the patties. Cook in oil for 3 minutes on each
side. Transfer to paper towel to cool.

1-5oz. Serving = 1 protein, 1/8 cooked vegetable scant grain, 1 Tbl oil

MUSSELS

2 lbs. Mussels
1 Garlic Clove
1 C. Tomato Sauce
1 Tbls. Lemon Juice
1 Tbls. Oregano
1 Tbls. Basil

Wash and remove beard from mussel. Combine other ingredients in large
saucepan, add 4 cups water, stir and simmer over medium heat for 3 minutes.
add mussels and simmer 7-10 minutes or until mussels open. Remove
mussels from pan. Pour base into 4 bowls and add 4 oz. of mussels. *Great
served with brown rice or quinoa*

5 oz. Serving = 1 protein; 1/4 C. cooked vegetable

SHRIMP AND SNOW PEA POD SOUP

4 C. Chicken Broth
1/4 tsp. Ginger
1/4 tsp. Onion Powder
1 C. Shrimp, cooked
1 C. Snow Pea Pods, fresh or frozen

Bring chicken broth, spices, pea pods to a boil. Add cooked, shelled shrimp until heated. Do not over cook; drain.
Pour broth over 4 oz shrimp and 1/2 C. snow peas
Serving = 1 protein, 1/2 cooked vegetable

Seafood

BAKED STUFFED FLOUNDER

12 oz. Flounder Fillets
6 Zucchini Slices
1/2 C. Mushrooms, sliced
4 Tomato Slices
pinch Mesquite Herbal Seasoning
1 tsp. Margarine

Combine vegetables and seasoning. Divide evenly between 2 fillets and top with 1/2 tsp. margarine each. Roll up fillets or fold end to end and fasten with a toothpick. Bake at 400° for 10 to 15 minutes
Yield: 2 servings
1/2 Recipe = 1 protein, 1/2 cup cooked vegetable

STUFFED FISH

4 Fish Fillets of choice
2 Tbls. Onion, chopped
1/4 C. Ricotta
1/4 C. Broccoli, chopped
1 tsp. Garlic Powder

1/2 tsp. Pepper
2 Tbls. Margarine, melted

Combine onion, ricotta, broccoli and seasonings. Stir to mix well. Divide mixture into 4 parts. Spread filling lengthwise on fish fillets. Fold fillets over filling, tucking fish under. Place the filled fish fillets, seam side down in a baking dish. Brush with melted margarine. Bake covered at 400° for about 30 minutes or until fish flakes apart easily when tested with a fork.

4 oz. = 1 protein, scant cooked vegetable, 1 tsp. oil

SHRIMP MARINARA OVER RICE

6 oz. Whole, Raw Shrimp
1/2 C. Tomatoes, chopped
1/4 C. Bell Peppers, chopped
1/4 C. Onion, chopped
1 Garlic Clove
Olive Oil
Salt, Pepper, Basil
1 C. Brown Rice, cooked

Peel and rinse shrimp. Saute vegetables in 1/2 Tbl. oil. Add shrimp and stir-fry until done, about 1-2 minutes depending on size. Season to taste and serve over rice. Also good served over Quinoa or Amaranth.

Recipe is 1 Serving = 1 protein, 1 grain, 1 cooked vegetable

CHANGE OF PACE FISH

5 oz. Fish
3/4 C. Mushrooms
1/4 C. Celery
1 Tbls. Lemon Juice
Oregano, Onion and Garlic to taste

Preheat oven to 350°. Place fish, topped with 1/2 vegetables and seasonings mixture in foil. Wrap tightly and bake 30 minutes.

1 Serving = 1 Protein and 1/2 C. cooked vegetable

BELGIAN ENDIVE WITH SALMON

2 C. Belgian Endive, whole leaves
1/4 C. Plain Nonfat Yogurt
1/4 C. Celery, minced
1 tsp. Onion Powder
2 Tbls. Fresh Dill Weed, minced
4 oz. Salmon, then cooked, chilled and flaked
Few drops hot pepper sauce.

Seafood

Wash endive and pat dry. Trim root ends and separate leaves. Combine yogurt, celery, onion powder and dill weed. Gently stir in salmon. Season to taste with hot pepper sauce. Pile mixture in shallow bowl and tuck endive leaves around edges.

Yield: 1 protein, 2 C. raw vegetables

Note: Salmon will be less than 1 serving but yogurt will complete it.

SALMON LOAF

1/2 C. Oat Bran
1/4 C. Hot Milk
1 (16 oz.) Can Salmon, flaked
1 tsp. Salt
1 tsp. Paprika
1/2 tsp. Lemon Rind, grated
1 Tbl. Lemon Juice
1 Egg
1 tsp. Hot Sauce

Combine bran and milk. Let soak 10 minutes. Add all other ingredients and mix lightly. Turn into a loaf pan that has been been coated with a non stick spray. Bake 1 hour at 325°. Yield: 4 servings.

6 oz = 1 protein, 1/4 C. grain

TUNA PATTIES

1 C. Zucchini (about 4 oz.), shredded
2 Tbls. Onion, chopped
1/2 tsp. Garlic Clove, minced
2 tsps. Margarine
12 oz. Tuna, packed in water, drained
2/3 C. Oatmeal or Oat Bran
1/4 tsp. Salt
1/4 tsp. Pepper

Saute zucchini, onion and garlic in 1 teaspoon margarine for about 5 minutes. Mix remaining ingredients until blended. Form into 8 patties and brown in 1 teaspoon of margarine in large skillet, over medium heat, about 3 minutes. Serve with lemon.

6 oz. Serving = 1/4 cup vegetable, 4 oz. protein, 1/2 serving grain, 1 tsp fat.

Seafood

LEMON CATFISH IN FOIL

12 oz. Catfish Fillets
4 tsps. Margarine
1/3 C. Lemon Juice
1 1/2 C. Carrots, diced
1/4 C. Celery, diced
1/4 C. Green Onion, chopped
2 tsps. Dried Parsley
2 Lemons, thinly sliced

Place catfish on a piece of foil that is about 4 inches longer than the fish. Melt margarine and add the lemon juice, pepper, carrots, celery, onions and parsley. Pour the mixture over the fish, dividing it evenly. Top the fish with the lemon slices. Bring the edges of the foil together and fold over several times. Twist one end of the foil to make it look like a fish tail. Tuck the other end under to form a point to make it look like the nose of the catfish. Place on flat sheet and bake at 350° for about 30 minutes or until fish flakes easily.

4 oz. fish = 1 protein, 1 teaspoon oil. Serve with 1 C. vegetables

NEW ORLEANS CATFISH

1 lb. Catfish
2 C. Cooked Brown Rice
2 Tbls. Onion, grated
1/2 tsp. Curry Powder
6 slices Lemon, sliced thinly
Fresh Parsley, chopped

Cut catfish into serving size pieces and place in a well greased baking dish. Sprinkle fish with salt and pepper. combine rice, onion & curry powder. Spread over the fish. Top with lemon slices and dot with margarine. Cover and bake at 350° for 25 to 35 minutes or until fish flakes with a fork. Remove cover the last few minutes of cooking to allow for slight browning. Sprinkle with parsley.

Servings: 4 oz. fish = 1 protein, 1 C. rice=1 grain

POACHED SOLE

5 oz. Sole
1/4 C. Fresh Celery Leaves
1/4 C. Peppercorns, chopped
Lemon slices
Paprika
Parsley

Place sole in skillet with 2 inches of gently simmering water flavored with 2 to 3 lemon slices, 1/4 cup chopped celery leaves and a few peppercorns. Simmer gently about 10 minutes. Remove fish from liquid and garnish with paprika and chopped fresh parsley.

Servings: 4 oz. = 1 protein

SHRIMP CHOW MEIN

8 oz. Small Whole Shrimp, cooked
1 C. Chopped Suey Vegetables, chopped & drained (or cooked mixed vegetables, such as oinions, cabbage, carrots, snow peas, red peppers and cauliflower)
1/2 C. Raw Mung Sprouts
1/2 C. Mushrooms, sliced
1/2 C. Celery, thinly sliced
1 tsp. Sesame Oil
1 C. Chicken Broth
2 Tbls. Wheat Free Tamari
1/2 tsp. Garlic Powder
2 C. Brown Rice or Millet

Combine all vegetables and seasonings, except mung sprouts. Cover and simmer in chicken broth on low heat 5 minutes. Add mung sprouts to cooked vegetables. Combine well. Serve over brown rice or millet.
Yield: 2 servings: 1 protein and 1 cooked vegetable

BOILED SHRIMP

2 lbs. raw Shrimp
8 C. Boiling Water
1-1/4 C. Onion, sliced
1 Garlic Clove
1 Bay Leaf
2 Ribs Celery
1 Tbls. Salt
1/8 tsp. Cayenne Pepper
1/2 Fresh Lemon, sliced thin,

De-vein, wash and drain shrimp. Add shrimp to water with the seasonings. Add lemon. Simmer shrimp for 3-5 minutes or until done. Cool in iced water. Drain and chill.
4 oz. shrimp = 1 protein

SALAD NICOISE

2 oz. White Tuna or Salmon
1 Hard Boiled Egg
6 oz. Baked Potato
1/2 C. Onion, chopped
1/2 C. Tomato
1 C. Lettuce or Spinach
1 tsp. Black Pepper
1 Tbls. Mustard Vinaigrette Dressing (recipe follows)

Peel potato, cut lengthwise and slice in perpendicular 1/4" pieces. Chop egg. Grill tuna if desired. Scatter chopped vegetables and egg on top of lettuce. Place tuna in center, in pieces on top of greens. Arrange potato slices in circle around lettuce, following circumference of plate. Add dressing and pepper.

**Yield: 1 protein serving, 1 raw vegetable, 1 starchy vegetable (grain,)
1 Tbl. dressing**

MUSTARD VINAIGRETTE DRESSING

1/2 C. Oil and Vinegar dressing
1 Tbl. Dijon Mustard
1/2 tsp. Pepper
Mix all ingredients with a wire whisk and chill.

BAKED SALMON STEAKS

1 Tbls. Cooking Oil
1 Tbls. Lemon Juice
1/2 tsp. Ground Ginger
Dash of Salt and Pepper
1 lb. Salmon Steak

Mix oil, lemon juice, ginger , salt and pepper. Brush mixture on salmon and refrigerate for 1 - 2 hours. Bake salmon at 400° until it flakes easily, about 10 to 15 minutes.

Yield: 3 servings. 4oz. serving = 1 protein

TUNA SQUARES

2 lbs. Canned Tuna
2 Eggs (or Egg Whites)
1/4 C. Oat Bran
2 Tbls. Lemon Juice
1/4 C. Pimento, chopped
1 medium size (take out seeds and discard) Green Pepper, chopped
1 Onion or 3 Green Onions, chopped
1 Carrot, grated

Mix all ingredients together. Pat into a greased 9" x 13" pan. Bake at 350°
for 25 minutes.

6 oz. = 1 protein, 1/4 C. cooked vegetables

ADDITIONAL RECIPES

Seafood

GRAINS AND STARCHES

WARNING!!!!!

Even if the recipe does not specifically state it, all ingredients in each and every recipe must be sugar, flour and wheat free.

Grains and Starches

BARLEY AND CORN MEDLEY

Saute or microwave together:
Summer Squash
Sweet Onion

Combine:
1 C. Cooked Barley
1/2 C. Cooked Corn
1 C. Squash mixture

Add:
1/4 tsp. Ground Thyme
Salt and pepper to taste
Garnish with parsley

Yield 1 Serving = 1 grain, 1 vegetable, 1 starchy vegetable

OVEN TOASTED POTATOES

1 large Baking Potato
Cooking Spray
Seasoned Pepper
Paprika

Scrub potato and cut into eight chunks. Place chunks in a non-stick baking pan. Spray lightly with non-stick spray. Sprinkle with a little seasoned pepper and paprika. Bake at 350° for 30 minutes or until fork tender and lightly browned.
Variation: Dip each piece in egg white and sprinkle with garlic seasoning and salt, or Old Bay Spices and salt.

Servings: 6 oz = 1 starchy vegetable

51

SOUTHERN POTATOES WITH CARROTS

Non-stick Cooking Spray
2 C. Carrots, peeled, cut in strips
1/2 C. Water
12 Oz.. Potatoes, peeled, cut into small strips
3 Tbls. Chopped Chives, fresh or dried
Dash of Ginger
Salt and Pepper

Spray wok with non stick cooking spray and heat on medium high. When the wok is hot, add the carrots and cook for 2 minutes stirring as needed. Add 1/4 C. of water, cover, and cook until liquid is absorbed. Add the potatoes, ginger, salt, pepper,and 1/4 C. water. Cover, and cook until liquid is absorbed (about 4 min.). Add the chives, toss and serve.

**Serving: 1 C. = 1/2 portion cooked vegetable
and 1 full portion starchy vegetable**

RICE & BARLEY PILAF

1 C. Raw Brown Rice
1/2 C. Raw Barley
1 C. Fresh Mushrooms, sliced
1 C. Celery, thinly sliced
1 C. Carrots, thinly sliced
1 C. Onion, minced
2 Garlic Cloves, minced
1/2 C. Fresh Parsley, chopped or 2 Tbls. dried
1 Tbls. Wheat Free Tamari
1/4 C. Pimentos

Cook brown rice & barley separately according to package directions. (Use 2 C. water for 1 C. rice and 3 C. water for 1 C. barley.) Saute garlic and onion in 1 Tbls. oil until soft. Add mushrooms and cook stirring gently for 3 to 5 minutes. Add chopped parsley. Steam carrots and celery until crisp-tender, 10-15 minutes. Combine: onion, mushroom mixture, carrot, celery mixture & grains. Add pimentos and tamari. Stir gently.

Serving, 1-1/2 cup = 1/2 grain, 1 vegetable

MILLET AND CAULIFLOWER

1 C. Millet
2 C. Cauliflower Flowerets
1 Onion, diced
3 C. Boiling Water
Sesame Oil
Pinch Sea Salt

Rinse Millet. Lightly brush a deep pot with a very small amount of oil. Saute onions in sesame oil for 2 minutes. Add boiling water and sea salt. Add millet, bring to a boil again. cover and reduce heat. Simmer for 30-35 minutes. Add cauliflower the last 5 minutes. Serve with a vegetarian protein such as baked tofu. Yield = 2 servings.

2 Cups = 1 grain, 1 cooked vegetable

CAJUN BEANS AND RICE

1 C. Cooked Pinto, Kidney or Red Beans
1 C. Brown Rice, cooked
1/4 tsp. Salt
1/4 C. Onion, chopped
1/4 C. Red Pepper, chopped
1 Clove Garlic, minced
1 Bay Leaf
1 tsp. Pepper

Combine all ingredients in a small saucepan. Simmer on medium heat for 5 minutes, stirring occasionally.

Yield: 1 serving= 1 grain, 1 protein, 1/2 Cup cooked vegetable

QUINOA AND BROCCOLI

1 C. Cooked Quinoa
1 C. Raw Broccoli flowerets, chopped
1 C. Turkey Broth (see soups)
Non-stick cooking spray
Salt and Pepper to taste

Spray small skillet with cooking spray. Add broccoli, cook on moderate heat, stir occasionally. Add turkey broth and simmer uncovered until broccoli is tender but firm. Add the Quinoa and stir. Serve hot.

Recipe = 1 cup grain and 1 cup cooked vegetable

BLACK-AND -RED CHILI

1/2 pound 93% Ultra-Lean Ground Beef
2 C. Onion, diced
1 C. Green Bell Pepper, chopped
1-1/2 Tbls. Chili Powder
2 tsps. Ground Cumin
1-1/2 tsps. Dried Oregano
1/4 tsp. Celery Seeds
3 (8 oz.) Cans, Sugar Free Tomato Sauce
1 (15-1/2 oz.) Can Red Beans, undrained
1 (15 oz.) Can Black Beans, undrained
1 (14-1/2 oz.) Can Whole Tomatoes, undrained and chopped

Cook meat in a large saucepan over medium heat until browned, stirring to crumble. Add onion and bell pepper; saute 3 minutes or until tender. Add chili powder and remaining ingredients; bring to a boil. Reduce heat and simmer, uncovered 30 minutes, stirring occasionally.

1 1/2 C. = 4 oz. protein and 1 cooked vegetable, 1 ounce sauce

GOURMET RICE BLEND

Bring 2 cups of water to a boil. Add 1 C. rice. Place lid on pan and reduce heat to low. Saute 1 C. carrots and 1 C. mushrooms in 2 tsp. margarine and add to cooked rice. Yield = 2 servings.

Serving: 2 C. Rice Blend = 1 grain, 1 C. cooked vegetable and 1 tsp oil.

BARLEY AND VEGETABLE CASSEROLE

2 C. Cooked Barley
1 tsp. Margarine
1 large Onion, chopped fine
1 C. Mushrooms, chopped fine
1 pound Shredded Zucchini
2 large Carrots, shredded
4 Large Egg Whites
1/2 tsp. Thyme
1 tsp. Dill
Sauce: 1 tsp. Dill Weed
      1 tsp. Lemon Rind
      1/2 C. Plain Yogurt

In a large skillet, saute onions, carrots, zucchini and mushrooms with margarine until onions are soft (about 4 minutes). Place vegetable mixture in a large bowl with the barley. Add egg whites, lemon rind, thyme and 1 tsp. dill and mix thoroughly. Spray casserole dish with non-stick cooking spray. Spoon in mixture from mixing bowl. Cover casserole; Bake for 40 min. at 350 °, uncover and bake 30 minutes more or until casserole is brown and pulls away from the side. Remove from oven and cool at room temp. Mix yogurt with the other tsp. dill. To serve-slice casserole and top with 2 tablespoons dill and yogurt mixture. Yield: 2 servings

1/2 Recipe = 1 grain, 2/3 cup cooked vegetable, 2 oz. protein.
2 tablespoons sauce

NEW ORLEANS DIRTY QUINOA

1 Tbls. Olive Oil
4 oz. Chicken Livers, finely chopped
1 C. Onion, chopped
3/4 C. Celery, diced
1/2 C. Green Bell Pepper, diced
2 Tbls. Chopped Shallots
1/2 lb. Sugar Free Bacon, chopped
2 large Cloves Garlic
1 Bay Leaf
3 C. Quinoa, uncooked
1/3 C. Water
1 Tbls. Tamari
2 tsps. Cajun Seasoning
1/4 tsp. Hot Sauce
3 C. Chicken Broth
1/2 C. Green Onions, sliced

Grains and Starches

Heat olive oil in a large saucepan over medium-low heat. Add chicken livers and saute 4 minutes or until done. Add onion and next 6 ingredients; saute 3 minutes or until vegetables are crisp-tender. Add quinoa and cook 2 minutes, stirring constantly. Add 1/3 cup water and next 4 ingredients; bring to a boil. Reduce heat and simmer, uncovered, 15 minutes or until liquid is absorbed, stirring occasionally. Remove bay leaf. Arrange on platter and sprinkle top with sliced green onion.

1 1/2 C. = 1 cup grain, 1/2 cup cooked vegetable, 3 oz. protein

BROWN RICE STUFFING

2 tsps. Margarine
2 medium tart, Red Apples, cored and diced
1/2 C. Onion, chopped
1/2 C. Celery, chopped
1/2 tsp. Poultry Seasoning
1/4 tsp. Dried Thyme leaves

1/4 tsp. Ground White Pepper
3 C. Brown Rice, cooked in 3 C. water and 3 C. of Chicken Broth

In a large skillet over medium-high heat, cook apples, onion, celery, and seasonings in margarine; cook until vegetables are tender crisp. Stir in cooked rice; continue cooking until heated through. Serve as stuffing with poultry or pork. Yield: 6 servings

1 Serving = 1 cup grain, 1/6 cup cooked vegetable, 1/3 cup fruit

BROWN RICE PILAF

1/2 C. Celery, chopped
1/2 C. Onion, chopped
1/2 C. Green Pepper, chopped
1/2 C. Carrots, chopped
1 Clove Garlic
3 Tbls. Oil
1/4 tsp. each of Paprika, Sage, Marjoram and Rosemary
1 C. Raw Brown Rice
2 C. Chicken or Beef Stock
1/2 tsp. Salt

Saute all the vegetables in the oil until the onions are golden and the celery is tender (about 10 minutes). Stir in the herbs and uncooked rice. Heat the stock, add to vegetable-rice mixture and bring to a boil. Lower heat, cover and simmer until all the liquid is absorbed and rice is tender, about 40 minutes.

Serving: 1 1/2 C. = 1 cup grain, 1/2 cup cooked vegetable,
1 1/2 teaspoon oil

MICROWAVE BAKED POTATO

Scrub an 8 ounce Potato well. Prick holes in it with a fork or other sharp object. Spray it with Cooking Spray. Bake in the microwave, on high, for 5 minutes. Turn it over and bake another 4 minutes.
Baking time will vary according to microwave power.

FRIED RICE

1/4 C. Onion, diced
1/4 C. Green Pepper, diced
1/4 C. Celery, diced
2 -3 Tbls. Oil
3 C. Long Grain Brown Rice, cooked 1 day in advance, (about 1 cup uncooked)
1/2 C. Green Peas (fresh or frozen), cooked
1 C. Chicken, cooked & diced
1 Egg Yolk, slightly beaten
2 Egg Whites, slightly beaten
1/4 C. Bean Sprouts (fresh or canned)
Wheat free Tamari (optional)

Grains and Starches

Saute onions, green pepper, celery in 2 tablespoons oil until just tender. Remove from pan. Add more oil to pan, if necessary, and saute rice. Add sauteed vegetables, peas, chicken and slightly-beaten eggs. Stir for 2 or 3 minutes or until eggs are set but not dry or brown. Add bean sprouts. Season with wheat free Tamari to taste.

Serving: 1 1/2 C. = 1 grain, 1/2 cup cooked vegetable, 2 oz. protein, 1 tablespoon oil

GRILLED SWEET POTATOES

4 Medium Sweet Potatoes
1/4 C. Liquid Egg Substitute or 1 egg white
1/4 tsp. Salt
Preheat oven to 425°

Scrub and cut sweet potatoes into quarters. Dip quarters into egg substitute and place on a shallow baking pan coated with non stick cooking spray. Bake for 20 to 25 minutes or until soft when pierced with a fork. Turn potatoes once during baking. Serve immediately.

6 oz. = 1 Starchy vegetable

SPAGHETTI SQUASH

1 (3-pound) Spaghetti Squash

Cut squash in half lengthwise; discard seeds. Place squash, cut side down, in a 13 x 9-inch baking dish. Add water to dish to a depth of 1/2 inch. Bake at 350° for 45 minutes or until squash is tender when pricked with a fork. Remove from water; let cool. Scrape inside of squash with the tines of a fork to remove spaghetti like strands.

Yield: 5 cups. 1/2 cup = 1 serving

MICROWAVE SPAGHETTI SQUASH

Cut squash in half lengthwise; discard the seeds. Place squash, cut side down, in a baking dish. Add 1/4 cup water to dish. Cover with heavy-duty plastic wrap and vent. Microwave at HIGH 15 minutes (or about 5 minutes per pound) until squash is tender when pricked with a fork.

SPAGHETTI SQUASH CASSEROLE

*1/2 C. Spaghetti Squash, steamed
**2 oz. Cooked Ground Turkey, seasoned to taste
3 Tbls. Part-Skim Ricotta or Cottage Cheese
1/2 C. Sugar Free Spaghetti Sauce

Preheat oven to 325°. Spray a 16 ounce casserole dish with vegetable coating. Simmer spaghetti sauce with meat for 15 minutes. Layer the following:

1/4 C. squash, ricotta cheese, 1/2 of meat sauce mixture, 1/4 C. squash, balance of meat sauce mixture. Bake until hot and bubbly, about 20 minutes.
* Eggplant, zucchini, broccoli or spinach may be substituted. Cook before measuring and adjust serving quantities.
**May eliminate turkey by substituting 1/2 cup (total) of part-skim ricotta or cottage cheese.

Yield 1 serving = 1 protein, 1/2 C. starchy vegetable, 1/2 C cooked vegetable. 6 oz. = 1 starchy vegetable

59

SQUASH WITH
BELL PEPPER SAUCE

2-1/2 C. Cooked Spaghetti Squash
1/3 C Green Onion
1/4 tsp. Dried Dillweed
1/8 tsp. Pepper
*Red Bell Pepper Sauce

Combine squash, green onions, dillweed and pepper; toss well. Serve with
*Red Bell Pepper Sauce. (recipe follows)
1/2 cup= 1 starchy vegetable*

RED BELL PEPPER SAUCE

2-3/4 C. Red Bell Pepper, chopped
1/4 C. Green Onions, chopped
1 Small Clove Garlic, minced
1/4 C. Water (or less)
2 Tbls.Tomato Paste
1/8 tsp. Salt
1/8 tsp. Pepper

Grains and Starches

Coat a large non stick skillet with cooking spray. Place over medium-high
heat until hot. Add bell pepper, green onions and garlic; saute 7 minutes or
until crisp-tender. Add water and remaining ingredients; cook 1 minute.
1/2 C. = 1/2 C cup cooked vegetable

SPAGHETTI SQUASH & RED CLAM SAUCE

1 (6-1/2-ounce) Can Minced Clams, undrained
1 Tbls. Olive Oil
1/2 C. Green Pepper, chopped
1/4 C. Green Onions, minced
4 Garlic Cloves, minced
2 Tbls. Tomato Paste
2 tsp. Dried Oregano
1 (14-1/2-ounce) Can Whole Tomatoes, undrained and chopped.

2 C. Cooked Spaghetti Squash
Fresh Oregano Sprigs (optional)

Drain clams, reserving liquid. Set clams aside. Heat oil in a large skillet over medium-high heat. Add bell pepper and next 2 ingredients; saute 5 minutes. Stir in reserved clam liquid, tomato paste, oregano and tomatoes; bring to a boil. Reduce heat and simmer, uncovered, 17 minutes or until reduced to 2 cups, stirring frequently. Remove from heat; stir in clams. Serve over 1/2 cup of spaghetti squash; garnish with fresh oregano, if desired.

1-1/4 C. sauce = 1 C. cooked vegetable, 3 oz. protein
1/2 C. spaghetti squash = 1 serving starchy vegetables

SPAGHETTI SQUASH PRIMAVERA

2 C. Spaghetti Squash, cooked
2 C. Broccoli Flowerets
1 C. Fresh Mushrooms, sliced
1 C. Yellow Squash, julienne-cut
1/4 C. Green Onions, sliced
1/2 (9-ounce) Package Frozen Sugar Snap Peas, thawed
2 Tbls. Balsamic Vinegar
2 tsps. Olive Oil
1 Tbls. chopped fresh Parsley
3/4 tsp. Dried Basil
1/8 tsp. Salt
1/8 tsp. Pepper
2 Garlic Cloves, crushed

Drop broccoli in a saucepan of boiling water; cook 1 minute. Drain. Combine broccoli and next 4 ingredients in a bowl; toss gently and set aside. Combine vinegar and oil in a small bowl, stir with a wire whisk until blended. Stir in parsley and next 3 ingredients. Add to vegetable mixture; toss well. Serve 1 C. over 1/2 C cooked spaghetti squash, chilled or at room temperature.

Serving = 1 C.cooked vegetable, 1/2 C. starchy vegetable

POTATO LATKES

6 Medium Potatoes
1 Onion, grated
2 Eggs, well beaten
3 Tbls. oatmeal
Salt and Pepper to taste
Vegetable Spray or (Margarine) for skillet

Peel and grate potatoes, place in large bowl of ice-water to keep them from turning brown. Squeeze dry and place in dry bowl. Add onion, eggs, oatmeal, salt and pepper. Mix well. Coat skillet with vegetable spray or (melted margarine) and drop mixture by large or small spoons full depending on the size latke you desire. Brown well on both sides and drain on paper towels.

1 Cup = 1 starchy vegetable, 1/2 protein (1 tsp fat)

ADDITIONAL RECIPES

VEGETABLES

Vegetables

WARNING!!!!!

Even if the recipe does not specifically state it, all ingredients in each and every recipe must be sugar, flour and wheat free.

Vegetables

COLE SLAW

1 head Cabbage, finely shredded
1/2 C. Carrots, diced
1/2 C. Green Pepper, diced
1 C. Celery, diced
1/2 C. Onion, diced
1/2 C. Pimento
2 Tbls. White Vinegar (or to taste)
1 Tbls. Mustard
Salt and Pepper

Soak cabbage and dry before using. Mix all vegetable ingredients. Next pour vinegar and mustard into a small bowl and mix. Use blender, if available, then pour over Cole slaw. Add salt and pepper to taste.

1 Cup = 1 cup raw vegetable

SPINACH AND MUSHROOM SALAD

1 lb. Raw Spinach, chopped
1 lb. Snow White Cap Mushrooms
1 Small Red Onion
1 Carrot, diced
Salt and Pepper

Wash spinach and mushrooms thoroughly and drain. Spinach should be chopped into small pieces and mushrooms should be sliced paper thin. Arrange in salad bowl, adding onion (thinly sliced) and diced carrots. Sprinkle salt and pepper to taste.

1 cup = 1 raw vegetable

ROMAINE, ENDIVE AND BEAN SALAD

1/4 C. Water
2-1/2 Tbls. Vinegar
1/2 tsp. Dried Oregano
1/4 tsp. Pepper
1 Clove Garlic, crushed
2 (16 oz.) Can Navy Beans, drained
6 C. Romaine Lettuce and tomato

Combine first 5 ingredients in a bowl, stirring with a wire whisk. Add beans; toss well and set aside. Arrange 1 cup romaine on each of 6 salad plates. Divide endive evenly among each serving. Mound 1/4 cup bean mixture in center of each salad evenly. Yield: 6 servings

1 C. = 1 raw vegetable, 1/2 C. starchy vegetable (or as 1/2 serving protein)

BAKED EGGPLANT AND TOMATOES

1 Medium Eggplant
1 (8 1/4 oz. can) Tomatoes, chopped
1/4 tsp. Garlic Powder
1/4 tsp. Dried Marjoram Leaves

Heat oven to 375°. Peel and slice eggplant into 1/2-inch slices. Cook in boiling water for 5-10 minutes or until just tender. Drain. Mix together tomatoes, marjoram and garlic powder. In a deep 1 quart casserole place a layer of 1/2 of the eggplant, 1/2 tomato mix. Repeat layers.

1 C. = 1 cup cooked vegetable.

RATATOUILLE

2 Medium Onions, peeled and sliced
1 Garlic Clove, minced
Olive Oil
2 Small Zucchini (one-pound size), washed and thinly sliced
2 Small Eggplants (one-pound size), peeled and cubed
2 Medium Green Peppers, washed; stem and seeds removed, cut into one inch strips
5 Medium Tomatoes, peeled and quartered, or
2 C. Canned Tomatoes, coarsely chopped
2 Tbls. Freshly Snipped Basil or
1/2 to 1 tsp. Dried Basil Leaves
2 Tbls. Fresh Parsley
1 tsp. Salt
1 tsp. Kelp Powder
1/4 tsp. Fresh Ground Pepper

Using a large, heavy skillet, saute onions and garlic in 1 tsp. olive oil for 5 minutes. Add zucchini, eggplant and green pepper to skillet, adding more oil as needed, use as little oil as possible. Stir gently, but thoroughly. Saute mixture for 10 minutes. Stir in the fresh or canned tomatoes, basil, parsley, salt, kelp powder and pepper. Reduce heat, cover skillet tightly and continue to simmer for 15 minutes longer. Serve immediately.

1 cup = 1 cooked vegetable

STUFFED EGGPLANT

2 Eggplants, split in half lengthwise
1 Medium-Sized Onion, chopped
1/2 Clove Garlic, minced
2 Tbls. Oil
1/2 lb. Cooked Beef, cut in small cubes
2 C. Tomatoes, fresh or canned
Salt to taste
1/2 tsp. Basil

Preheat oven to 350°.
Scoop pulp from eggplant halves, leaving 1/2-inch shell. Dice pulp. Saute onion, garlic and eggplant pulp in oil. Add cubed, cooked meat, tomatoes, salt to taste and basil. Fill eggplant shells with mixture. Put water 1/2 inch deep in bottom of baking pan. Add filled eggplant halves, cover with foil and bake at 350° for 1/2 hour. Uncover and continue baking until shell is tender enough to eat, about 20 minutes. Yield: 4 servings

1 Serving = 2 cup cooked vegetable, 2 oz. protein, 1 1/2 teaspoon oil

SAUTEED PEPPERS

1 C. Green Pepper, thinly sliced
1 C. Red Pepper, thinly sliced
1/4 C. Onion, thinly sliced
Twist of Lemon Juice

In a non stick pan, saute onion until clear and soft; not browned. Add peppers and saute 3-5 minutes until softened. Sprinkle with lemon juice.

Yield: 2 C. cooked vegetable

Vegetables

GREEN BEANS IN CROCK POT

1 Lb. Green Beans, fresh
2 Garlic Cloves, fresh
2 Fresh Tomatoes, coarsely chopped
Pepper to taste
Cook in crock pot until tender.

1 Cup = 1 cup cooked vegetable.

RED CABBAGE

2 Tbls. Oil
1 Tbls. Onion, chopped fine
2 tart Cooking Apples, cored and thinly sliced
2 Tbls. Lemon Juice or Cider Vinegar
1/2 C. Water
1 head Red Cabbage (2 lbs.), cored and thinly shredded
1 tsp. Salt
1/4 tsp. Caraway Seeds (optional)

Heat oil in a large skillet over medium heat. Saute onion until golden. Add sliced apple, lemon juice or cider vinegar, water and cabbage. Stir thoroughly to combine. Season with salt. Add caraway seeds, if desired. Cover tightly and simmer over low heat for 15-20 minutes, stirring occasionally. Remove from heat and serve immediately.

1 Cup = 1 cooked vegetable

Vegetables

ASPARAGUS & BEET SALAD

Look for Golden Beets at Farmer's Markets, wonderfully sweet. They will not bleed into the other ingredients the way red ones do. If you cannot find very thin stalks of asparagus, cut thicker asparagus lengthwise in halves or quarters after peeling.

1 lb Small Beets (6-8) preferably a mixture of Red and Golden, washed, tops trimmed.
2 lbs. Thin Asparagus
Salt to taste
1 Large Shallot, finely chopped
2 Tbls. Balsamic Vinegar
Freshly Ground Black Pepper to taste.
1/4 C. Extra-Virgin Oil

Preheat oven to 375°. Place beets in a baking dish, if using red and golden beets, bake them separately. Add 1/2 C. water, cover tightly with aluminum foil. Bake for about 1 hr. or until the beets are tender when pierced with a knife. Let stand until cool enough to handle. Peel off skin. Cut the beets into quarters or eighths, depending on their size. Snap off tough ends of asparagus stalks. Peel lower portion of asparagus stalks, cut into 3 inch lengths. In large pot of boiling, salted water, cook asparagus until just tender, about 1-2 minutes. Drain; refresh with cold water. Pat dry. In a small bowl, stir together shallots, vinegar, salt and pepper. Gradually, whisk in oil. In a medium-size bowl toss the beets with half of the shallot vinaigrette, If using different colors of beets use separate bowls. Taste and adjust seasoning. Arrange the beets and asparagus on individual plates.

1 Cup = 1 Cooked vegetable, 2 tsp. oil.

BAKED BEETS

1 Pound Fresh Beets, tops removed and washed
1 Tbls. Fresh Dill, chopped
1 Tbls. Margarine or oil
Salt and Pepper to taste

Wrap each beet in foil and bake at 375° until tender, about 1 hour. Cool beets. Unwrap, peel,and slice. In a hot skillet melt the Margarine or oil, add the beets, dill, salt and pepper, cook for 3 min.

1 C. = 1 cup cooked vegetable, 1 teaspoon oil

DILLED GREEN BEANS

1 Lb Fresh Green Beans
1 tsp. Margarine
2 tsp. Lemon Juice
2 Tbls. Fresh Dill, chopped
Salt and Pepper to taste

Rinse and trim beans. Steam or boil beans for 6 minutes, then drain. In a saucepan, melt the butter, add the beans and cook for 2 minutes on medium heat. Add the dill, lemon, salt and pepper; toss and serve.

1 C. = 1 cooked vegetable

BROCCOLI-CAULIFLOWER SALAD

1/2 C. Raw Broccoli
1/2 C. Raw Cauliflower
1 Tbl. chopped Red Onion
2 Tbl. Vinegar and Oil dressing
Toss ingredients together lightly.

Yield: 1 C. raw vegetable, 1 oil

BAKED MUSHROOM

1/2 C. Mushrooms, sliced thin
Non Stick Cooking Spray

Spray baking sheet with cooking spray. Place the mushrooms on baking sheet in a single layer. Bake mushrooms in oven at 275° for 2 -2 1/2 hours, until dry.

Makes 1/2 Cup serving of vegetable

69

HOT PICKLED BEETS

3/4 C. Canned Beets, drained
3 Slices Bermuda Onion
1/2 C. Herbed Vinegar Dressing, or Italian Dressing

Mix vegetables with dressing and marinate overnight in refrigerator. Enjoy cold or heat before serving. Drain before serving. Yield: 1 serving.
1 cup cooked vegetable, 2 tablespoons dressing

ROASTED GREEN BEANS WITH BABY ONIONS

1 Qt Water
8 Oz. Baby White Onion
2 Lbs. Green Beans, cleaned and ends trimmed
2 Tbls. Extra-Virgin Olive Oil
10 Cloves Garlic, peeled
1/2 tsp. Sea Salt
Freshly ground Black Pepper
1 Tbls. Balsamic Vinegar

Bring water to a boil in a medium saucepan. Drop in onions and let cook 2-3 minutes until skins loosen. Strain onions in a colander. When cool enough to handle, peel onions with your fingers.

Preheat oven to 375°. In a 9" X 13" baking dish, combine onions, green beans and garlic. Sprinkle with salt. Pour olive oil over and toss evenly to coat vegetables.

Bake vegetables 2-3 minutes, stirring occasionally, until crisp tender. Remove from oven and drizzle with vinegar, season to taste with black pepper.
1 Cup serving = 1 cup cooked vegetable, 1 tsp. oil

Vegetables

70

SQUASH ITALIAN STYLE

1 C. Plum Tomatoes, chopped
1 Garlic Clove, chopped
2 tsp. Fresh Parsley, chopped
1/2 tsp. Oregano
2 tsp. Fresh Parsley, chopped
1/2 tsp. Oregano
1 Medium Summer Squash, 1/4 inch thick slices
Salt and Pepper to taste
1/4 C. Tomato Juice

Combine all of the ingredients except squash. Put the squash in a microwave dish and toss with the tomato mixture. Cover microwave dish and place in microwave oven. Microwave on high for 3 minutes. Stir, then microwave for 3 more minutes.

1 C. = 1 cup cooked vegetable

TOMATO AND WAX BEANS

1 Lb. Fresh Yellow Wax Beans, washed, and trimmed
1 Clove Garlic, crushed
1 Tbls. Olive Oil
Salt and Pepper to taste
1/4 C. Water
2 Tbls. Fresh Basil, chopped
3 Medium Fresh Tomatoes, chopped
Combine all ingredients.

1 C. = 1 cup cooked vegetables, 1 teaspoon oil

EGGPLANT SALAD

Cube peeled eggplant. Soak in salted water for 5 minutes, rinse well. Put in Microwave dish with enough water to cover bottom of dish and cook for ten (10) minutes on High setting. Add a prepared Tomato and Basil Sauce or other prepared Marinara Sauce that is sugar free. Serve Hot or cold.

1 cup = 1 cup cooked vegetable.

Vegetables

CARAWAY CABBAGE

2 C. Red Cabbage, chopped
1/2 C. Onion, sliced
1 Tbls. Vinegar
1/4 C. Balsamic Vinegar
1 tsp. Caraway Seed
Place ingredients in saucepan with 2 cups water. Simmer on medium for 10 minutes, until cabbage is soft but not mushy. Drain water and serve.

1 Cup = 1 cooked vegetable

SPINACH FLORENTINE

1 lb Fresh Spinach
1 Medium Red Onion
1 Medium Tomato
4 Large Mushrooms
1 Tbls. Margarine
1 tsp. Basil
1 tsp. Oregano
1/2 tsp. Black Pepper
1/2 C. Skim Milk Ricotta Cheese

Wash spinach and cut stems off. Slice onion, mushrooms and chop tomato. Melt margarine in large saucepan. Add basil, oregano and pepper. Add vegetables to pan and simmer over medium heat, stirring occasionally until spinach becomes mushy. Add ricotta cheese and stir. Cooking time should take approximately 10 minutes. Transfer to serving.

1 Cup = 1 cooked vegetable, 1 oz. protein

Vegetables

ZUCCHINI WITH MINT

Non-Stick Cooking Spray
1 C. Onions, diced
2 C. Zucchini, cut into thin strips
1 tsp. Fresh Spearmint, chopped
1 tsp. Fresh Peppermint, chopped
(Option: use 1 tsp. of dried mint flakes in place of fresh mint)

Spray skillet with non-stick cooking spray. Add onions. Place on high heat. Cook until onions are clear. Add zucchini, stir, and reduce heat. Cover and cook until zucchini is tender, about 3 minutes or until onions are clear.

1 C. = 1 cooked vegetable

RAINBOW PEPPER MEDLEY

2 Green Peppers
2 Sweet Red Peppers
1 Sweet Yellow Pepper
1 Purple Onion (optional)
1/3 C. Vegetable Oil
2 Tbls. Tarragon Vinegar
1 Tbls. Dijon Mustard
1 tsp. Salt
1/4 tsp. Ground Pepper
1/4 tsp. Hot Sauce(optional)
1 Jalapeno Pepper, minced (optional)
2 tsps. Caraway Seeds
1 tsp. Lime Rind, grated

Cut peppers and onion into julienne strips; set aside. Combine oil and next 6 ingredients in a large bowl. Beat with a wire whisk until thickened. Add reserved vegetables, jalapeno pepper, caraway seeds and lime rind, tossing gently. Cover and refrigerate at least 3 hours. Drain well before serving. Well covered and refrigerated it will last for days.

1 Cup = 1 cup raw vegetables, 1/2 tsp. oil

Vegetables

CURRIED CABBAGE

1 Large Head Green Cabbage
1 Onion, chopped
2 Tbls. Mustard Seed
2 fresh Chilies, chopped (optional)
1 tsp. Cumin, ground
1-1/2 tsp. Chili Powder
2 Tbls. Oil
Salt to taste

Cut cabbage head in quarters, remove core and slice as thin as possible. Saute onions and spices in oil, starting with a small amount and add more oil as you need it. Add cabbage and toss lightly in skillet until tender. Salt to taste. Serve immediately. *Cover pan with lid while mustard seeds cook, to keep them from "popping" out of the pan.

1 cup = 1 cooked vegetable, 1/2 tsp. oil

HEALTH SALAD

1 Head Cabbage, finely shredded
2 Medium Carrots, shredded
1 Medium Green Pepper, finely chopped
1 Small Red Onion, thinly sliced
2 Tbls. Cider vinegar (or to taste)
1/4 C. Corn Oil
1/2 tsp. Celery Seed
1/4 tsp. Garlic Powder
1/4 tsp. Salt

Toss together first four items. In small bowl, mix together the next five items. Pour over cabbage mixture. Cover and refrigerate overnight.

1 Cup = 1 cup raw vegetable, 1 tsp. oil

CURRIED CAULIFLOWER SALAD

4 C. Fresh Cauliflower Flowerets, sliced (about 14 oz.)
1/4 C. Plain Nonfat Yogurt
2 Tbls. Mayonnaise
1/2 tsp. Curry Powder
1/8 tsp. Salt
1/8 tsp. Coarsely Ground Pepper
2 Tbl. Fresh Parsley, chopped

Arrange cauliflower in a vegetable steamer over boiling water. Cover and steam 4 minutes or until crisp-tender. Place cauliflower in a large bowl; let cool 10 minutes. Combine yogurt and next 4 ingredients; stir well with a wire whisk. Pour over cauliflower and toss gently to coat. Add parsley and toss again.

Yield: 4 servings. 1 cup = 1 cooked vegetable, 1 ounce sauce

STRING BEAN STUFFING

1 pkg. French Cut String Beans
1 pkg. Cauliflower, cooked and mashed
1 lb. Mushrooms, sliced
1 Onion, chopped
Chicken or Vegetable Broth
Tamari Sauce

Saute onion, string beans, and mushrooms in a small amount of broth. Stir in cauliflower. Stuff into poultry.

1 C. serving = 1 cup cooked vegetable

Vegetables

75

FLORENTINE SQUASH BAKE

1/8 tsp. Ground Red Pepper
2 C. Skim Milk
Vegetable Cooking Spray
1/2 C. Onion, chopped
3 Garlic Cloves, minced
1 pkg.(10 oz.) Frozen Chopped Spinach, thawed,
drained and squeezed dry
5 C. Cooked Spaghetti Squash
2/3 C. Sugar Free Salami, or any left over meat,chopped

Place ground red pepper in a bowl with milk.
Coat a large saucepan with cooking spray and place over medium-high heat until hot. Add onion and garlic; saute 1 minute. Add milk mixture Add spinach; stir well. Remove from heat; stir in squash and meat. Spoon mixture into a 13 x 9 inch casserole coated with cooking spray. Bake at 375° for 20 minutes.

2 cups = 1/2 cup starchy vegetable, 1 cup cooked vegetable,
4 oz. protein

Vegetables

ROASTED VEGETABLES

4 Large unpeeled potatoes
1 Medium Red Onion, cut into 6 wedges
3 Tbls. Vegetable Oil
Salt
2 Bunches baby carrots, peeled
1/2 Lb. Baby Pattypan Squash or Yellow Straightneck Squash, cut into bite-sized chunks
1/2 Lb. Green Beans, stems trimmed
2 Large Red Peppers, cut into 2-inch chunks
2 Large Yellow Peppers, cut into 2-inch chunks
1 Tbl. Freshly minced Thyme, or 1 tsp. dried Thyme Leaves
1/2 tsp Coarsely Ground Black Pepper
1 Large Lemon, slices

Preheat oven to 425°. In large roasting pan (about 17" x 11-1/2"), toss potatoes and onion with 1 tablespoon vegetable oil and 1/2 teaspoon salt. Roast 15 minutes.

Add carrots squash, green beans, red and yellow peppers, thyme, black pepper, 2 tablespoons vegetable oil, 1 teaspoon salt and half the lemon slices. Continue roasting 45 minutes, turning vegetables with pancake turner twice, until vegetables are golden and tender.

Arrange vegetables on platter; garnish with remaining lemon slices. Separate potatoes from other vegetables in order to distinguish the starchy vegetable from the regular.

Experiment with different spices, such as, rosemary, mint, garlic, etc.

**6 ounce potato = 1 starchy vegetable, 1 cup vegetable = 1 vegetable,
1 1/2 teaspoon oil**

Vegetables

ADDITIONAL RECIPES

Vegetables

POULTRY

WARNING!!!!!

Even if the recipe does not specifically state it, all ingredients in each and every recipe must be sugar, flour and wheat free.

GRILLED CHICKEN SPINACH SALAD

5 oz Boneless Chicken Breast
1/2 C. of combined Mushrooms, Tomatoes, and Onions,
1/2 C.Spinach
2 Tbls. Light Wheat Free Tamari sauce
1/4 tsp. Ground Ginger
1 Tbls. Vinaigrette Dressing

Cut chicken breast into small pieces. Marinate in Tamari sauce and ginger for 30 minutes. Grill in skillet until done. Arrange 1/2 cup of assorted vegetables on top of 1/2 cup of spinach. Add chicken. Top with dressing.
Serving = 4 oz. protein, 1 C. raw vegetable, 1/2 Tbl. oil

LEMON BARBECUED CHICKEN

2 Chicken Breast Halves or Thighs and Legs
1/2 tsp. Lemon rind, grated
3/4 tsp. Salt
1/4 tsp. Dry Mustard
1/4 tsp. Dried Oregano
1/4 C. Lemon Juice
1/4 C. Salad Oil
1 Tbl. Scallions, chopped
1/2 tsp. Wheat free Tamari

Poultry

Mix lemon rind, salt, dry mustard, oregano and Tamari in a small bowl. Gradually stir in lemon juice, then oil and scallions. Pour over chicken in large bowl; marinate in refrigerator for 2 hours. Remove chicken from marinade and place skin-side down on grill. Set 3 to 6 inches from charcoal that has reached light gray stage. Cook for 45 minutes to 1 hour, turning once.
4 oz = 1 protein, 1 teaspoon oil

MEXICAN TURKEY BURGERS

1 lb. Ground Turkey Breast
1 Tbl. Chili Powder or Mexican Seasoning
2 Tbls. Minced Garlic
Fresh Ground Black Pepper to taste

Mix all ingredients together and form into 4 patties. Broil or grill approximately 5 minutes on each side or until done. Good crumbled on salad and served with Salsa.

4 oz.= 1 protein

TURKEY (CHICKEN) LOAF

1 lb. Ground Turkey or Ground Chicken
3 Eggs
Soy Powder (Sugar free, or other sugar-free protein powder)
Salt and Pepper to taste
1/4 tsp. Tarragon

Mix ground turkey or chicken, eggs, seasonings and just enough soy powder to hold loaf together. Bake covered at 400° for 35 minutes.

4 oz. = 1 protein

SALSA CHICKEN

2 - 3 lbs Chicken Legs & Thighs
1 (8 oz) can Tomato sauce
1 C. Salsa
Salt & Pepper
Garlic or Garlic Powder
Brown chicken pieces. Drain fat. Pour tomato sauce, salsa, salt, pepper and garlic over chicken. Simmer for 45 minutes.
Use sauce as a cooked vegetable over rice, quinoa, barley, etc.

4 oz (usually 2-3 pieces) = 1 protein

SPANISH CHICKEN AND RICE

4 oz. Cooked and Boned Chicken
1 C. Canned Tomatoes, diced
1 Small Onion, diced
1 tsp. Oil
1 C. Brown Rice,
1/2 tsp. Thyme
1 tsp.Parsley
1/2 tsp. Garlic Powder
1/4 tsp. Pepper

Cook rice according to directions. Saute onion in oil. Add remaining ingredients including brown rice and simmer 15 minutes.

Serving: 4 oz. protein, 1 C. grain, 1 C. cooked vegetable

SUNDAY CHICKEN

1 Small stalk Celery, sliced 1/2-inch thick
4 (5 oz.) Chicken Breast Halves, de-boned and skinned
Salt and Pepper to taste
4 C. fresh Mashed Potatoes made with extra Milk so that they are practically liquid. Start with 1 cup Skim Milk and add as needed

Preheat oven 450°. Lightly oil or use non stick cooking spray to coat a 10-inch cast-iron frying pan; add chicken breasts, meaty side up; sprinkle with salt and pepper. Thin fresh mashed potatoes with extra milk until almost liquid. Pour potato mixture over chicken. Bake 20-25 minutes or until potatoes are nicely brown. For a nice crunchiness, substitute water chestnuts for the celery. Dish can also be made with bone-in turkey or chicken breasts but add 10 minutes to baking time.

Serving: 4 oz. protein, 1/2 starchy vegetable

Poultry

CHICKEN CHILI

3 Tbls. Olive Oil

2 medium Onions, chopped

3 Garlic Cloves, finely chopped

2 1/2 Tbls. Chili Powder

2 tsp. Ground cumin

1 tsp. Dried Oregano Leaves crushed

1/4 tsp. Cayenne Pepper; or to taste

1 3/4 C. Chicken Broth

1 (28 oz) Can Italian peeled Tomatoes, chopped, with juice

1 1/2 c. Water

1 tsp. Salt

1 Bay Leaf

2 lbs. Boneless, Skinless Chicken Breasts cut into 1-inch chunks

2 medium Zucchini (1 to 1 1/4 lbs.), cut into cubes

1 (15 to 16 oz.) can Black or White Beans rinsed and drained

1 (11 oz.) can Whole-Kernel Corn, drained

In stock pot with cover, heat olive oil over medium heat. Add onions, cover and cook 5 minutes. Uncover and continue to cook, stirring occasionally, another 8-10 minutes or until onions are pale golden and just beginning to brown. Add garlic, chili powder, cumin, oregano and cayenne. Cook, stirring, 1-2 minutes to toast spices lightly, but do not let them burn. Stir in chicken broth. Add tomatoes and juice, water, salt and bay leaf. Bring to a boil over high heat, reduce heat to low and simmer, partially covered, 40 minutes. Remove bay leaf. (Recipe can be prepared to this point up to two days ahead and refrigerated. When ready to finish, return chili base to gentle boil.) Add chicken and zucchini, bring to boil; reduce heat and simmer 5 minutes; add beans and corn, simmer 5 minutes more or until heated through.

Serving size: 2 cups = 1 protein, 1 cooked vegetable, 1 starchy vegetable, 1 tsp oil

Poultry

82

CHICKEN CACCIATORE

3 lbs Frying Chicken, cut in serving size pieces
1/2 C. Onion, chopped
1/4 C. Green Pepper, chopped
1/2 C. Celery, chopped
1 (20 oz.) canned Tomatoes
1/2 tsp. Salt
1 Clove Garlic, minced
1 tsp. Parsley Flakes
Dash Oregano

Brown pieces of chicken in skillet sprayed with non stick vegetable cooking spray. Add vegetables, salt and spices. Cover and simmer 1 hour. Mix together.
4 ounces chicken = 1 protein 1 Cup sauce= 1 cooked vegetable

TURKEY SPREAD

Non Stick Cooking Spray
1/2 pound Ground Turkey
1/8 tsp. Salt 1/8 tsp. Pepper
3 Tbls. Low-Fat plain Yogurt
1 med. Onion chopped
pinch Paprika
pinch Nutmeg

Poultry

Spray skillet with cooking spray, and brown the turkey, salt, and pepper until the turkey is completely cooked. Blend the turkey, and the remaining ingredients in a food processor, or blender for 30 seconds on high. Place in a small bowl and chill for at least 2 hours. Delicious on rice cakes.
4-ounces = 1 protein

BASIL CHICKEN MEDLEY

1 Tbl. Olive Oil
3 Garlic Cloves, minced
2 Whole Skinless, Boneless Chicken Breasts (about 1-1/4 lbs), cut into 1-inch chunks
1 C. Zucchini, cut into chunks
1 C. Tomatoes, cut into chunks
1 Tbl. Dried Basil
2 Tbls. Vinegar
1/4 tsp. Pepper
5 C. Brown Rice, cooked

Heat oil in a skillet; Add chicken and cook until no longer pink; remove and keep warm. In a separate bowl combine zucchini, tomato, basil and vinegar; toss to coat vegetables well. Add to skillet and stir fry about 3-5 minutes. Weigh 4 ounces chicken, place on platter with, 1 cup cooked brown rice, top with 1/2 cup vegetables.

Serving: 1 C. grain, 4 oz. protein, 1/2 C. cooked vegetable

DILLED CHICKEN AND RICE SALAD

4 C. Brown Rice, cooked
2 C. Chicken Breast, cooked and diced (about 1 lb)
3/4 C. Green Onions, sliced
1 C. Carrot, diced
1/4 C. Mayonnaise
2 Tbls. Fresh Dillweed, chopped
1/2 tsp. Salt
1/2 tsp. Coarsely Ground Pepper
1 Tbls. Dijon Mustard
1 Tbls. Lemon Juice
8 oz. Plain Nonfat Yogurt
Fresh Dillweed Sprigs (optional)

Combine first 4 ingredients in a bowl; toss gently. In another small bowl combine mayonnaise and next 6 ingredients; stir well. Add to rice mixture, toss to coat. Garnish with fresh dill sprigs if desired. Yield: 4 servings

1 1/2 C= 1 protein, 1 grain, 1 Tbls. oil

TURKEY & APPLE SAUSAGE PATTIES
Great for breakfast.

2 tsp. Vegetable oil
1 Onion, finely chopped
2 C. Tart Apples, such as Granny Smith, grated
1 lb. Ground Turkey
1 C. Oatmeal or Oat bran
2 large Egg Whites
2 tsp. Rubbed Dried Sage
1-1/2 tsp. Salt
1/4 tsp. Black Pepper, freshly ground
1/4 tsp. Nutmeg, freshly grated
1/4 tsp. Allspice

Preheat oven to 450°. Spray a baking sheet with non stick cooking spray or line it with parchment paper. In non stick skillet, heat oil over medium heat. Add onions and saute until softened, about 3 minutes. Add apples and saute for 3 to 5 minutes longer or until the apples are very tender. Transfer to a large bowl and let cool completely. Add turkey, oatmeal (or bran), egg whites, sage, salt, pepper, nutmeg and allspice; mix well. Divide the sausage mixture into 16 portions and form into 3/4-inch patties. (the patties can be prepared ahead and stored or baked and stored , well wrapped, in the freezer for up to 3 months). Place the patties on the prepared baking sheet and bake until the outside is golden brown and the interior is no longer pink, about 10 minutes for fresh patties or 20 minutes for frozen patties. The easy way: Just mix all of the ingredients raw,form into patties and bake according to directions.

3 patties = 1 protein, 1/2 fruit, 1/4 grain

Poultry

85

HERBED CHICKEN

3/4 C. Plain Nonfat Yogurt
1/2 tsp. Dried Whole Basil
1/2 tsp. Dried Whole Oregano
1/2 tsp. Dried Whole Thyme
1/8 tsp. Pepper
1 Tbl Lemon Juice
1 clove Garlic, minced
4 (5 oz) Chicken Breast Halves, skinned and boned
Vegetable Cooking Spray

Combine first 8 ingredients in a shallow dish; stir well. Add chicken, turning to coat. Cover and marinate in refrigerator 1 hour. Remove chicken from marinade, reserving marinade. Place chicken on a rack coated with cooking spray; place rack in a broiler pan. Broil 5-1/2 inches away from heat 10 minutes on each side or until done, basting occasionally with reserved marinade.   **4 oz. = 1 protein**

SPANISH RICE WITH CHICKEN AND PEPPERS

1 Tbls. Vegetable Oil
2 C. Brown Rice, uncooked
1-1/3 C. Onion, chopped
1 C. (1 inch) squares Green Bell Pepper
1 C. (1 inch) squares Red Bell Pepper
1/2 tsp. Dried Oregano
1/2 tsp.Ground Cumin
1 large clove Garlic, minced
2 C. Chicken Broth
1 lb. Chicken Thighs, skinned, boned and cut in 1/2 inch cubes
Salt & Pepper

Heat oil in a large saucepan over medium heat. Add rice; saute 9 minutes or until golden. Add onion and next 5 ingredients; saute 3 minutes or until crisp-tender. Add chicken broth and next 2 ingredients; bring to boil. Add chicken; bring to boil. Cover, reduce heat and simmer 15 minutes or until liquid is absorbed.   Yield: 4- 1-1/2 cup servings

1 Serving = 1 protein, 1 grain, 1/2 cooked vegetable

BEEF OR TURKEY CHILI WITH BEANS

2 lbs. Lean Ground Beef or Ground Turkey Breast
1 Large Green Pepper, chopped
1 Large Onion, chopped
1 (28 oz) Can Tomatoes, chopped and drained
1(18 oz) Can Tomato Paste
1 Can Tomato Puree
1 (19 oz) Can Red Kidney Beans, drained
3 Tbls. Chili Powder
2 tsp.Salt
5 dashes Tabasco Pepper Sauce - to suit your taste.

Cook meat, green pepper and onion in large skillet over medium heat until browned, stirring to crumble. Drain, put in crock pot. Add remaining ingredients. Cook overnight or all day, or put all ingredients in a large pot, bring to a boil, reduce heat and simmer 2 hours.
2 Cups = 1 complete dinner

CHICKEN AND THREE PEPPERS SALAD

4 oz. Chicken, cooked and cut in cubes
1 C. Green, Red or Yellow Pepper, cut into bite-sized pieces
2 Tbls. Olive Oil
2 tsp. White Vinegar
1/2 tsp. Dried Basil Leaves, crushed
1/4 tsp. Dried Oregano Leaves, crushed
1 medium Clove Garlic, minced
1 C. Salad Greens

Poultry

In a medium bowl, gently stir together chicken and peppers. In a cup stir together olive oil, vinegar, basil, oregano and garlic. Pour dressing over chicken and peppers. Toss gently and serve on salad greens.Yield: 1 Serving
Recipe = 1 protein, 1 cup raw vegetable

GREEN BEAN AND CHICKEN STROGANOFF

2 Tbls. Oil
1 Lb. Whole Chicken Breasts, skinned, halved, boned and cut crosswise into 1/4-inch strips
2 C. Fresh, canned or frozen(thawed) Green Beans, cut into 1- 1/2-inch pieces
1 Medium Onion, thinly sliced
1 Garlic Clove, minced
1/2 C. Mushrooms, sliced
1 C. Chicken Broth
8 oz. Low Fat Yogurt
1/8 tsp. White Pepper
4 C. Cooked Brown Rice

Heat oil in large skillet over medium-high heat. Cook chicken in oil until no longer pink. Remove from skillet; keep warm. Add green beans, onion, garlic and mushrooms to skillet; stir-fry until vegetables are crisp-tender. Stir in chicken broth; heat to boiling. In a small bowl, blend yogurt and pepper; stir into broth mixture. Reduce heat to low; cook and stir until mixture thickens. Add chicken; cook and stir until thoroughly heated (DO NOT BOIL). Serve over rice. Yield: 4 servings.

1 Chicken breast = 1 protein + 1 C. cooked vegetables
1 Cup rice = 1 grain 2 Tbl Sauce = 1 serving sauce

Poultry

MICROWAVE DIRECTIONS: Place chicken in 2-Qt. microwave-safe casserole. Cover with waxed paper and microwave on HIGH for 6 to 10 minutes or until chicken is no longer pink, stirring once halfway through cooking. Drain chicken and remove; keep warm. In casserole, combine 1 Tbls. oil, green beans, onion, garlic and mushrooms. Cover and microwave on HIGH for 5 to 7 minutes or until beans are crisp-tender, stirring once halfway through cooking. In a small bowl, combine chicken broth and pepper; stir into vegetable mixture.

Microwave on HIGH for 4 to 5 minutes or until mixture thickens and boils,stirring once halfway through cooking. Stir in chicken and yogurt. cover and microwave on medium for 3 to 4 minutes or until thoroughly heated (DO NOT BOIL), stirring once halfway through cooking. Serve over rice.

1 Chicken breast = 1 protein + 1 C. cooked vegetables
1 Cup rice = 1 grain 2 Tbl Sauce = 1 serving sauce

CHINESE CHICKEN FRIED RICE

3 tsps. Vegetable Oil, divided
12 oz.. Chicken Breasts, skinned, boned and cut into strips
2 tsps. Ginger, minced and peeled
1 Garlic Clove, chopped
1-1/4 C. Onion, slivered
3 C. Cooked Brown Rice
1 Egg slightly beaten
2 Tbls. Wheat-Free Tamari
1/4 tsp. Salt
Romaine Lettuce, thinly sliced
Green Onions, sliced

Heat 1-1/2 tsp. vegetable oil in skillet over high heat. Add chicken; saute 2 minutes or until done. Remove from skillet; set aside; keep warm. Add the remaining 1-1/2 tsp. of vegetable oil to skillet over medium-high heat. Add ginger root and garlic; saute 10 seconds. Add onion and saute 1 minute. Add rice; saute 2 minutes. Stir in slightly beaten egg into rice mixture; saute 1 minute. Add Tamari and salt; cook an additional 30 seconds. For each serving use 1 Cup rice mixture and 4 oz chicken. Serve warm over 1 cup lettuce and green onion.

1 Serving = 1 grain, 1 protein, 1/3 C cooked vegetable, 1 tsp oil

CAJUN TURKEY VEGETABLE LOAF

2 lbs. Ground Turkey Breast (99% Lean)
1 (10 oz.) pkg. Frozen Chopped Spinach, thawed and well drained
1/2 C. Onion, finely chopped
1/2 C. Red or Green Bell Pepper, chopped
1/2 C. Carrots, shredded
4 Egg Whites, slightly beaten
2 Tbls. Water
2 tsp. Ground Cumin
2 tsp. Dried Oregano
1 tsp. Dried Thyme
1 tsp. Paprika
1 tsp. Salt (optional)
1/8 tsp. Crushed Red Pepper Flakes

Heat oven to 350°. Lightly spray a 13 x 9 inch baking dish with non stick cooking spray or grease lightly. Combine all ingredients; mix lightly but thoroughly. Place in prepared baking dish and shape into a 9 x 6-inch loaf. Bake 1 hour or until juices run clear. Let stand 10 minutes and serve. Yield: 10 servings

8 oz. = 1 protein, 1/2 cup vegetables

TURKEY BROTH

Bones left over from a roast turkey
2 Tbls. Poultry Seasoning
1 Tbls. Celery Seed
1 Tbls. Dried Parsley
1 Garlic Clove, minced
1/2 tsp. Pepper
2 Tbls. Salt

Poultry

Put bones in a large cooking pot. Cover completely with water. Add all remaining ingredients and bring to a boil. Reduce heat and simmer for 2 hours. Remove from heat, cool and strain broth into large bowl. Refrigerate over night. The next day skim fat off top of broth and throw fat away. Spoon broth into freezer bags and freeze up to 6 months for use in other recipes.

CHICKEN DINNER IN A DISH

4 (5 oz.)Whole Chicken Breasts, skinned, boned
2 Medium Potatoes, quartered
2 Carrots, cut into 2-inch pieces
1 large Onion, cut into wedges
1/2 C. Chicken Broth
1 Bay Leaf
Salt and Pepper to taste
1 pkg. (8 oz) Frozen Cut Green Beans, thawed and drained

Heat oven to 350°. In ungreased 12 x 8-inch (2-Quart) baking dish, arrange chicken, potatoes, carrots and onion. Pour broth over chicken; add bay leaf. Sprinkle with salt and pepper. Cover with foil. Bake at 350° for one hour. Add beans to chicken and vegetables. Cover and bake for an additional 10 - 15 minutes or until chicken is fork tender and juices run clear and vegetables are tender.

**For each serving use
4 oz. Chicken = 1 protein,
6oz C. potato = 1 starchy vegetable.
1C. Cooked vegetables**

Poultry

91

SOUP

WARNING!!!!!

Even if the recipe does not specifically state it, all ingredients in each and every recipe must be sugar, flour and wheat free.

Soup

TOMATO SOUP

1 16 oz. Can Chicken Broth
1 28 oz. Can Whole, Peeled, Plum Tomatoes
2 Medium Potatoes, peeled and chopped
1/2 C. Onion, chopped
1/4 tsp. Nutmeg
1/4 tsp. Ginger
1 Tbl. Orange Rind, grated
1 Cinnamon Stick
Mint Leaves or Parsley as garnish

Spray large, deep pan with non-stick coating. Saute chopped onion until tender about 5 minutes. Season with ginger and nutmeg. Add orange rind. Add tomatoes without sugar, chicken broth, cinnamon stick, and potatoes. Salt and pepper to taste. Bring to a boil, cover and let simmer for 1 hour. When cool, remove cinnamon stick, put mixture in blender until creamy. Serve hot with parsley or mint leaves as garnish. This makes a creamy, thick soup without dairy or a thickener.

Serving: 2 C. = 1 starchy vegetable and 1 cooked vegetable.

BUTTERNUT-CAULIFLOWER SOUP
(creamy soup with no dairy or oil)

1 Small Onion, chopped
1 Small Butternut Squash, peeled and diced
1/2 Head Cauliflower, chopped
4 C. Water
1/2 C. Rolled Oats
Salt to taste
White Pepper to taste

Combine all ingredients in heavy soup pot. Bring to a boil. Reduce heat and simmer for 30 minutes. Puree in blender or with hand blender.

1 C. = 1/2 C. cooked vegetable, 1/2 C. starchy vegetable, 1/4 C grain

Soup

93

BARLEY SOUP

1 Tbls. Oil
1 lb. Lean Chuck Roast of Beef, cut into one-inch cubes
1 lb. Soup Bone
1-1/2 Qts. Water
2 Tbls. Parsley, chopped
Salt to taste
2 Tbls. Paprika
2 Peppercorns
1 1/2 Whole Allspice or 1 tsp. ground Allspice
2 C. Raw Barley
1 C. Celery, chopped, with leaves
1 C. Onion, chopped
1 C. Carrots, diced
1 C. Fresh or Canned Tomatoes
Parsley for garnish

Put one tablespoon oil in a heavy six-quart container with cover. Place container over medium heat and lightly brown beef cubes and soup bone. Add water and bring to a boil, skimming surface as needed. Add parsley, salt, paprika, peppercorns and allspice. Reduce heat to low, cover and simmer for 30 minutes. Add remaining ingredients and simmer another 30 to 40 minutes.

2 C. = 1 protein, 1 cooked vegetable, 1 grain

AUTUMN SOUP

2 Butternut Squash
2 Sweet Potatoes
1 Medium Onion
1 Carrot
1 Celery Stalk
1-1/2 quarts Vegetable Stock or Water
1 Tbl. Olive Oil

Soup

94

2 tsp.. Coriander
1 tsp. Nutmeg
1 tsp. Cardamom
1 tsp. White Pepper

Peel and dice sweet potatoes and squash. Dice carrot, onion, celery and saute in olive oil. Add vegetable stock, squash and sweet potato. Bring to a boil; add seasoning. Reduce heat and simmer until done, about 2 hours. Remove from heat and cool. Puree in food processor. Return to simmer and adjust seasonings.

1/2 Cup = 1 starchy vegetable

BLACK BEAN SOUP

1/2 lb. Dried Black Beans
1 Quart Water
1-1/2 tsp. Salt
1 Tbls. Olive Oil
1 C. Onions, chopped
1/2 C. Green Pepper, chopped (optional)
1 tsp. Garlic, minced
1/2 tsp. Ground Cumin
1/2 tsp. Oregano
1/8 tsp. Dry Mustard
1-1/2 tsp. Lemon Juice

Presoak beans in water overnight or use quick-cooking method on pack. After soaking beans, add 1 teaspoon of the salt and bring to a boil; cover and simmer on low heat for 2 hours. Heat oil, add onions and saute until onions are tender.

Stir in remaining ingredients. Add about 3/4 cup hot bean liquid, cover and simmer 10 minutes. Add onion seasoning mixture to beans and continue to cook 1 hour, stirring occasionally. Top with chopped onion.

1/2 Cup = 1 cup starchy vegetable

Soup

TURKEY BARLEY SOUP

2 C. Cooked turkey, diced
2 C. Cooked Barley
1 C. Carrots, sliced thick
1/2 C. Broccoli Stems, chopped
2 Medium Onions, cut in wedges
1/2 C. of Celery, chopped
8 C. Turkey Broth
1/2 tsp. Poultry Seasoning
Salt and Pepper to taste

Pour turkey broth into large sauce pan. Bring to a boil over moderate heat, then reduce heat and simmer. Add carrots, cover and cook 10 minutes. Add broccoli, celery and onions and cook for 2 minutes. Add remaining ingredients, stir, and simmer 2 minutes.

2 C. = 1 protein, 1 grain, 1 cooked vegetable

SPICY TOMATO SOUP

1 Tbl. Olive Oil
2 C. Onion, chopped
2 tsp. Orange Rind, grated
5 Garlic Cloves, minced
1-1/2 tsp. Ground Cumin
1 tsp. Dried Whole Basil
1/2 to 1-1/2 tsps. Crushed Red Pepper
4- (14-1/2 oz) Cans Tomatoes, undrained and chopped
2-1/2 C. Chicken Broth

Heat oil in a large saucepan over medium heat. Add onion, orange rind and garlic; saute 8 minutes or until onion is tender. Add cumin, basil and red pepper; saute 1 minute. Add tomatoes and chicken broth; bring to a boil. Reduce heat and simmer, uncovered, 30 minutes.

1 Cup = 1 cooked vegetable

Soup

SUCCOTASH SOUP

1-1/2 C. Dried Baby Lima Beans
1 C. Water
3 C. Chicken Broth
1 Tbl. Vegetable Oil
1 C. Onion, chopped
3/4 C. Bell Pepper, chopped
1/2 C. Celery, chopped
3/4 C. Green Onions, chopped
2-1/2 tsp. Dried Whole Thyme
1/2 tsp. Salt
1/4 tsp. Pepper
dash of Red Pepper
1 (14-1/2 oz) Can Whole Tomatoes, undrained and chopped
2 C. Frozen Whole Kernel Corn

Sort and wash beans; place in a large Dutch oven. Cover with water to 2 inches above beans; bring to a boil and cook 2 minutes. Remove from heat; cover and let stand 1 hour.

Drain beans; add 1 cup water and broth. Bring to a boil; cover, reduce heat and simmer 40 minutes or until beans are tender. Heat vegetable oil in a large skillet over medium-high heat. Add onion; saute 2 minutes. Add bell pepper and celery; saute 2 minutes. Add green onions; saute 1 minute. Add onion mixture, thyme and remaining ingredients to bean mixture; bring to a boil. Cover, reduce heat and simmer 20 min.

1 1/2 C. = 1/2 cup cooked vegetable, 1 starchy vegetable

Soup

BEEF AND ONION SOUP

1 large Spanish Onion, cut into wedges
1 (1 lb.) Pot Roast, cut into cubes
1 Tbl. Parsley
1 Garlic Clove, crushed
2 C. Water
1 Tbl. Onion Salt
Pepper to taste
Non-Stick Cooking Spray

Spray a skillet with non-stick cooking spray. Add onions, cook until clear. Remove onions from skillet and set aside. Add beef to the skillet and brown on high heat until all sides are cooked. Add garlic and saute for 1 minute. Add water and simmer for 20 minutes. Add onions and all remaining ingredients, simmer until meat is tender, about 20 minutes.

4 oz. meat = 1 protein, 1 cup onions and broth = 1 cooked vegetable

TOMATO-BASIL BISQUE

2 tsp Olive or Salad Oil
2 Medium-sized Carrots
1 Large stalk Celery
1 Medium-size onion, chopped
3/4 tsp. salt
1 Clove Garlic, minced
1-1/2 Lbs. ripe tomatoes, peeled, seeded and coarsely chopped
1 C. V-8 juice
1/2 C. Loosely packed basil leaves, finely chopped
Basil sprigs for garnish

Cook carrots, celery, onion, and salt over medium heat in a non-stick 10-inch skillet with the oil, stirring frequently, until vegetables are tender but not browned, about 15 minutes. Add garlic; cook, stirring constantly, 1 minute. In blender or food processor with knife blade attached, puree vegetable mixture, tomatoes, V-8 juice and 1 cup cold water in batches, if necessary, until smooth. Pour soup into large bowl; stir in chopped basil. Cover and refrigerate until ready to serve. Garnish with basil sprigs.

1 Cup = 1 cooked vegetable

MAIN DISHES

WARNING!!!!!

Even if the recipe does not specifically state it, all ingredients in each and every recipe must be sugar, flour and wheat free.

MEATLOAF

1-1/2 lbs. Lean Ground Beef
1 C. Oat Bran
2 Eggs
1 (8oz.) Can Tomato Sauce
1/2 C. Onion, chopped
2 Tbls. Green Pepper, chopped
1-1/2 tsp. Salt
1 Medium Bay Leaf, crushed
Dash Thyme
Dash Marjoram

Preheat oven to 350°. Combine all ingredients; mix well.   Pat into a 9-inch loaf pan. Bake for 1 hour.

5oz. = 1 protein , 1/4 grain

LAMB STUFFED EGGPLANT

1 Small Eggplant
1 C. each, Onion, Bell Pepper, Tomato, chopped
2 Cloves Garlic, chopped
1 Tbl. Olive Oil
10 oz. Raw Ground Lamb
2/3 C. Raw Rolled Oats
Salt, Pepper
Cinnamon, Basil, Cumin to taste

Bake eggplant until soft, (about 8 minutes on high in the microwave). Cut in half lengthwise. Scrape out inside and chop, leaving skin intact. Cook lamb in skillet. Drain fat. Saute chopped vegetables and garlic in olive oil until onions are transparent. Mix 1 cup chopped eggplant, sauteed vegetables, drained meat, oatmeal and spices. Pile into eggplant skins and bake at 400° for 30 minutes.

1/2 Recipe = 1 protein, 1 cooked vegetable, 1/2 grain

Main
Dishes

99

STIR-FRY

5 oz. Chicken, Tofu (6 oz), Shrimp, Scallops or Beef
1 C. Brown Rice
1-1/2 C. Vegetables (Bok-Choy,, Snow Peas, Pea Pods, Green Onions,
Green Pepper, Broccoli etc.), all chopped
1 Tbls. Hot Sesame Oil
1 Tbls. Light wheat-free Tamari
1 Garlic Clove, minced
1 tsp. Fresh Ginger, minced
1 tsp. Pepper

Cut chicken (or other protein) in bite size pieces and marinate in Tamari sauce for one hour before grilling. Heat oil in skillet or wok. Add garlic and ginger. Grill chicken until cooked 3/4 done. Place aside in dish. Add vegetables to skillet; stir fry for 3 minutes. Add chicken and pepper to vegetables. Stir-fry 3 minutes. Serve over 1 cup brown rice.

4 oz. chicken (6 oz. tofu)= 1 protein
1 C. vegetable = 1 cooked vegetable
1 Tbl oil

VEAL AND PEPPERS ITALIANO

1 Lb. Veal
1 (10-1/2 oz.) Can Tomato Puree
1 Garlic Clove, minced
1/2 tsp. Dried Basil, crushed
1/2 tsp Oregano, crushed
3/4 tsp. Salt (optional)
1/8 tsp. Pepper
2 Green Peppers, sliced in strips
1 Medium Onion, sliced
2-1/2 C. hot, cooked Brown Rice

Trim fat from veal. Cut into 1-inch cubes and brown in skillet that has been sprayed with non-stick vegetable spray. Stir in tomato

Main
Dishes

puree and spices. Simmer, covered, 25 minutes. Add green peppers and onions. Cook, covered, 20 minutes. Serve over rice.

4 oz. Veal = 1 protein
1/2 C. Vegetables and tomato sauce= 1 cooked vegetable.
1 C. Rice = 1 grain

MEATBALL STROGANOFF

1 lb. Ground Sirloin
1/2 C. Oat Bran
1 tsp. Margarine
2 tsps. Onion, minced
1 tsp. Salt
Dash of Ground Pepper
Dash of Ground Cloves
Dash of Ground Nutmeg
6 Tbls. Skim Milk
Vegetable Cooking Spray
1 Tbls. Margarine
1-1/2 C. Beef Broth
1/2 C.Yogurt

Combine first 9 ingredients in a bowl and stir well. Shape mixture into 24 (1-inch) balls; set meatballs aside. Coat a large non-stick skillet with cooking spray; add margarine and place skillet over medium heat until margarine melts. Add meatballs from skillet; set aside and keep warm. Wipe drippings from pan with a paper towel. Gradually add beef broth. Cook over medium heat for 3 minutes. Remove from heat and stir in yogurt. Return the meatballs to skillet and cook for 3 minutes or until thoroughly heated. Serve over brown rice or barley

1 Cup rice = 1 grain. 4 oz meatballs = 1 protein.
2 Tbl sauce = 1 serving sauce

101

PENNSYLVANIA POT ROAST

Vegetable Cooking Spray
1 (1-1/2 lbs.) Beef Eye of Round Roast
3/4 C. Beef Broth
1 C. Onion, chopped
1/2 C. Canned, Undrained, Tomatoes, crushed
1/4 C. Carrots, diced
1/4 C. Celery, diced
1/4 C. Turnips, diced
2 Tbl Fresh Parsley, chopped
1/4 tsp. Dried Thyme
4 Black Peppercorns
1 Bay Leaf
Fresh Parsley Sprigs (optional)

Coat a large saucepan with cooking spray; place over medium-high heat until hot. Add roast, browning on all sides. Add broth and next 9 ingredients to pan; bring to a boil. Cover, reduce heat and simmer 3 hours or until tender. Slice roast and place on a serving platter; set aside and keep warm. Increase heat to medium and cook with mixture, uncovered, 10 minutes or until reduced to 1-2/3 cups. Discard peppercorns and bay leaf. Serve sauce with roast. Garnish with fresh parsley.

4 oz. beef = 1 protein, 1 C. sauce = 1 cup cooked vegetable

LAMB SHANKS IN DILL SAUCE

4 Lamb Shanks (3-4 lbs) with bones
2 Garlic Cloves, minced
1 Large Onion, chopped
2 Tbls. Lemon Juice
Salt and Pepper
1/2 lb. Mushrooms, cut in large pieces

1 C. Chicken or Veal Broth
1/2 Pint Yogurt, at room temperature
1 Tbls. Fresh Dill, finely chopped

Soak a 3 quart clay cooker for 15 minutes. Place the shanks in the pot. Combine the garlic, onion, parsley, lemon juice, salt & pepper and spoon it over the meat. Add the mushrooms and broth. Cover the pot and place it in a cold oven. Set the oven at 400° and cook 1 to 1 1/2 hours or until the meat is tender.

Pour the lamb juices into a small saucepan and boil until they are reduced to about 1 cup. Mix 1/2 cup yogurt stirring until it is smooth. Whisk mixture into the pan juices. Add the dill and simmer over low heat just until the sauce is heated through. Spoon the sauce over the meat.

4 oz. = 1 protein. 2 Tbl sauce = 1 serving sauce

ITALIAN SWISS STEAK

1 lb. Swiss Steaks
1 tsp. Garlic Powder
1 C. Green Pepper, chopped
1 C. Onions, chopped
1 Large Tomato, sliced thin

In a large skillet, fry the steaks on both sides until brown. Add all the ingredients except tomatoes. Cover skillet and simmer for 8 minutes. Remove steaks and place on a serving platter. Top with tomato slices. Pour the sauce over the steaks and tomatoes and serve.

4 oz. steak = 1 protein. 1 cup vegetables = 1 cooked vegetable

103

MEXICAN SAUSAGE

16 oz. Spicy Italian Sausage
2 C. Frozen Whole Kernel Corn
1 C. Brown Rice
4. C. Tomato Juice
1 Tbls. Chili Powder
1/2 C. Peppers, diced

In a large skillet, brown the sausage. Slice cooked sausage, in rings. Drain off the fat. Add all the remaining ingredients. Simmer until brown rice is tender, about 40 minutes.
Serving: 2 cups = 1 protein, 1/2 starchy vegetable, 1/2 grain, 1/4 cup cooked vegetable

NEW ENGLAND BEEF BOIL

4 lbs. Corned Beef Brisket,(be sure to check brine for sugar) rinsed
6 White Boiling Onions, peeled
4 Medium Turnips, peeled
6 Red Boiling potatoes, scrubbed
6 Small Carrots, peeled and cut in 1-inch pieces
1 lb. White Cabbage, cut into wedges.

MUSTARD SAUCE (optional)
1/3 C. Prepared Mustard
1 Tbl. Prepared Horseradish

Place corned beef in a 6-1/2 quart Dutch oven; cover with cold water. Bring to a boil; reduce heat and simmer for 2-1/2 to 3 hours or until almost tender. Turn beef once and skim off foam if necessary. Add onions and turnips; cook for 30 minutes. Add potatoes, carrots and cabbage. Cook for 20 minutes or until meat and vegetables are tender. Trim fat from beef; slice. Combine mustard and horseradish and serve with beef and vegetables, if desired.
4 oz. corned beef = 1 protein, 1 Cup turnip = 1 starchy vegetable, 1 Cup vegetables = 1 cooked vegetable

YANKEE POT ROAST

2 Lbs. Bottom Round Roast
3 C. Tomato Juice
2 C. Onion, thinly sliced
2 Garlic Cloves,minced
1/4 tsp. each, Black Pepper and Salt
1 tsp. each Basil,Thyme,
1/2 C. Mushrooms, sliced
1/2 C. Marjoram
2 Tbls. Parsley, chopped
Non Stick Cooking Spray

Preheat oven to 325°. Season the roast with the salt and pepper and place on a broiler pan. Broil roast, turning as needed until all sides are brown. Combine onion, tomato juice, and spices in a 5 qt. Dutch oven, bring to a boil. Add the roast, cover, and bake for 2 1/2 to 3 hours or until tender. Spray a skillet with cooking spray, add mushrooms, and stir until brown. Remove the roast; slice, and place on a platter with slices overlapping. Puree the vegetable mixture, add to mushrooms, mix well and pour over meat. Sprinkle with parsley, and serve.

4 oz. roast with 1/2 cup mushroom mix = 1 protein and 1/2 cup cooked vegetable

SPICY SAUSAGE AND POTATOES

3 C. Baked Potatoes, peeled and cubed
3 C. Italian Sausage, cooked & sliced
1/4 C. Onions, diced
3 Tbls. Parsley Flakes
1/4 C. Italian Dressing

Mix all the ingredients in a large bowl. Refrigerate for 2 or more hours and serve.

2 cups = 1 protein and 1 C. starchy vegetable.

PAT'S PROGRAM PORK SUPREME

6 oz. Pork Chop or 5 oz. Boneless Pork Chop
5 Green Onion stalks
1 Small Zucchini
1/2 C. Red Cabbage
1/4 C.Salsa
Dash of garlic powder or more to taste

Saute onion and zucchini in non-stick pan or in non-alcoholic spray Add 1/4 cup water. Cover and let simmer until tender. Add Salsa. Add pork chop and cook over low heat until done, about 5-7 minutes or until tender. Serve with salad.

Recipe = 1 protein, 1 cooked vegetable

ROAST BEEF

3 pound Sirloin Tips, Top or Bottom Round Rump Roast, Boneless Chuck Roast, etc.
Several (4) Bay Leaves
Tamari
Fresh or Powdered Garlic.

Cover meat with wheat free Tamari, fresh chopped garlic or garlic powder to taste. Lay bay leaves on top. Bake at 250° until tender, basting occasionally.

4 oz. = 1 protein

PEPPER STEAK

6 oz. Beef Round, sliced and cut into strips
2 Green Peppers, cut into strips
1 Medium Onion, chopped
2 C. Sugar Free Beef Stock
1 Tbl. Wheat Free Tamari sauce
1/2 tsp. Garlic Powder

Brown beef in skillet. Add stock, onion and spices. Simmer 1 hour. Add green pepper after 45 minutes.

Serving: 4 oz. = 1 protein, 1/2 cup cooked vegetable

ADDITIONAL RECIPES

METABOLIC ADJUSTMENT

BAKED FRUIT

1 Medium Apple or other firm fruit
1/2 tsp. Cinnamon
1 tsp. Margarine (optional)

Core fruit and slice into 8 equal slices. Place in a microwave safe container, sprinkle cinnamon over fruit and cook 4-5 minutes on high power. (Optional...Melt margarine in microwave for 20 seconds. pour over fruit and serve.)

Recipe = 1 fruit, 1 teaspoon oil

WARNING!!!!!

Even if the recipe does not specifically state it, all ingredients in each and every recipe must be sugar, flour and wheat free.

MA

ADDITIONAL RECIPES

INDEX
(Alphabetically by Category and Recipe)

BREAKFAST

CONDIMENTS

GRAINS AND STARCHES

MAIN DISHES

METABOLIC ADJUSTMENT

SEAFOOD

VEGETABLES

VEGETARIAN DISHES

Notes and Additional Recipes